D0351130

ENGLISH OUR ENGLISH

(*and how to sing it*)

KEITH WATERHOUSE

VIKING

VIKING
Published by the Penguin Group
Penguin Books Ltd, 27 Wrights Lane, London W8 5TZ,
England
Penguin Books USA Inc., 375 Hudson Street, New York,
New York 10014, USA
Penguin Books Australia Ltd, Ringwood, Victoria,
Australia
Penguin Books Canada Ltd, 2801 John Street,
Markham, Ontario, Canada L3R 1B4
Penguin Books (NZ) Ltd, 182–190 Wairau Road,
Auckland 10, New Zealand

Penguin Books Ltd, Registered Offices:
Harmondsworth, Middlesex, England

First published in Great Britain by Viking 1991
10 9 8 7 6 5 4

Copyright © Keith Waterhouse Ltd, 1991

The moral right of the author has been asserted

All rights reserved. Without limiting the rights under
copyright reserved above, no part of this publication
may be reproduced, stored in or introduced into a
retrieval system, or transmitted, in any form or by any
means (electronic, mechanical, photocopying, recording
or otherwise), without the prior written permission of
both the copyright owner and the above publisher of
this book.

Filmset in Linotronic Palatino by Wyvern Typesetting Ltd,
Bristol

Printed and bound in Great Britain by
BPCC Hazells Ltd
Member of BPCC Ltd

A CIP catalogue record for this book is available from
the British Library

ISBN 0-670-83269-3

Contents

Introduction

Mythology has it that there was once a golden age of English teaching, when every ten year old could parse a sentence and write a properly punctuated essay free of grammatical errors and spelling mistakes, and in copperplate too, in between learning 'Drake's Drum' and 'There's a breathless hush in the Close to-night' by heart.

The legend does not bear too close a look. The 1921 Newbolt Report on the teaching of English, so we are reminded by its successor the Bullock Report over half a century later, contains a catalogue of complaints from employers about the poor educational quality of the school leavers sent to them. Vickers Ltd reported 'great difficulty in obtaining junior clerks who can speak and write English clearly and correctly'. Lever Bros recorded their surprise and disappointment over young employees 'hopelessly deficient' in their command of English. Boots Pure Drug Co. observed that 'teaching of English in the present day schools produces a very limited command of the English language'.

They were talking, though, about school leavers aged fourteen or fifteen. It is doubtful whether seventy years ago examiners in higher education were noting, as they were in the late 1980s, that 'students nearing the end of degree courses are found to have insufficient command of English and show an inability to communicate their ideas at a level suitable for students about to obtain their degrees'.

Is this evident decline the result of higher education now being more widely accessible, or of teaching standards having dropped – or, to make a chicken and egg question of it, have teaching standards dropped because there has to be a greater supply of higher education to meet the demand ('More means worse')?

Educators hostile to formal grammar teaching strongly insist that there is nothing very much wrong with the state of the language, and to prove it they produce statistics showing that more pupils than ever before are now obtaining what used to be called an O-level pass in English. Sceptics accuse them of lowering the hurdles, of reducing attainment tests to a caucus race where everybody wins – or rather nobody loses, which is not quite the same thing.

The truth seems to be, as Orwell put it somewhat ahead of Prince Charles, that 'most people who bother with the matter at all would admit that the English language is in a bad way'. That was in 1946. The evidence may still be only anecdotal, as the experts claim, yet the anecdotes are by now coming in thick and fast. A fraction of one day's crop: the roadworks with its sign *Pedestrian's this-way*; the bank advertisement *What's orange, got three legs and eats melons?*; the newly painted concrete pillars in the House of Commons car park with the chalk-scrawled warning *Wet paint on the Pillow's*; the London Underground poster *If you evade your fare you could be fined up to £400 or more and get a criminal record which will effect the rest of your life*; the reported existence of a *funfare* on Brighton pier; the newspaper playing ducks and drakes with plural and singular *Drought restrictions and a spiralling cost of living has forced hotels to take action*; the building society slogan *Everything comes to he who waits*; the film poster *A movie with a lovers beat to it's pulse*. And so on. Go back only two or three decades into the files and such howlers are hard to find.

One reason often put forward for all this visible sub-literacy and sloppiness is that girls who at one time would have been scullery maids are now audio-typists, while lads who might have been factory hands are now local government clerks – that with de-industrialization and the growth of the service industries and of the public sector, more and more workers are required to use writing skills, or what passes for them, which at one time would have been tested only in their private letters home to mother. However depressing this variation on the more-means-worse theme – school leavers stretched beyond their abilities will fail to meet the expectations of their employers – there is probably something in it. Yet it fails to explain why syntactical blunders are now so common in even the most serious newspapers and journals that the day has long gone when they could be passed off as printers' errors. If journalists, who trade in words, have an imperfect command of the language, it can only be because they were imperfectly taught it.

Some would say that the rot set in back in the late Fifties when clause analysis or parsing – the naming of parts such as subject, verb, object – was abolished from O-level English, and a way of teaching grammar using terminology going back to the dawn of education began to wither away. In its place came 'language in use' – the notion that children should learn about the language from the language itself, from their own reading – newspapers and magazines as well as literature – and from classroom dialogue.

It is now often said, with political hindsight, that the switch was more ideological than educational – a growing hostility by a new generation of teachers in an increasingly multi-ethnic environment towards white middle-class 'elitism'. That is altogether too sweeping. Those were heady times: we were at the threshold of the so-called swinging

Sixties when the walls of deference came tumbling down. In the liberated, anti-establishment spirit of the period, teachers were themselves taught that the discipline of grammar taught in isolation from English studies was the worst sort of gradgrindery, of little or no use in improving writing skills.

There was something to be said for this outlook. There is no proof that an acquaintance with grammatical terms leads to improved language use any more than – to use an analogy familiar to linguists – knowing how to strip down an internal combustion engine is an aid to better driving. But the knowledge that the pedal on the right is called the accelerator, the one in the middle is the brake and the one on the left is the clutch is essential to the learner driver. His instructor may whimsically give them easier names – the fast pedal, the slow pedal, the change pedal – but he still has to know what they are called as well as what they are for, if he is to learn how to drive within the year. In their enthusiasm for lively 'English in use' in place of dead clause analysis, many teachers placed themselves in the position of driving instructors trying to demonstrate the hill start and the three-point turn while omitting to identify the hand brake and gear lever.

Such was their determination not to burden pupils with terminology that from a refusal to teach the rules of grammar evolved a disinclination even to correct grammatical errors, in the belief that what the pupil had to say was more important than the way in which it was said, so long as it could be understood and that the writer had 'communicated'. The proper use of apostrophes and commas, of principles such as that of number (a verb has to agree with its subject: the wine merchant should not boast that *A wide selection of spirits are always available*), went out of the window. As the years passed by, the system began to turn out teachers who themselves knew little grammar or sentence structure. Members of the 1988 Kingman Committee on the teaching of English language, when visiting a teacher training college, were asked by a bewildered student (now a primary school teacher), 'What's this syntax you all keep banging on about?' We reached the absurd point where a professor of linguistics, wishing to demonstrate to first-year students why the old-style rule 'Never end a sentence with a preposition' was far too prescriptive for these enlightened days, found that he first had to explain what a preposition was.

The new approach produced a good deal of creative writing, including an over-abundance of non-rhyming poems composed entirely of nouns and participles (*Wind blowing, leaves swirling* etc.) and written on sugar paper. It encouraged children to explore their language far beyond the stepping stones of their textbooks, although they may have felt somewhat hampered when required to analyse different types of writing without access to analytical tools. (In their study of the peculiar language of advertising, their innate knowledge of English, to which we are coming presently, will tell them that *Before you sample Hamburg's nightlife. Drink in the scenery* is a sentence chopped in two, like a worm. They probably know, without prompting, how to put it right – turn the stop into a comma. But do they know what is wrong with it?) It certainly brought a breath of fresh air into the English class. What it emphatically did not do was to raise the general level of literacy. Rather, it lowered it, and below the Plimsoll line at that.

But what did it all matter anyway? What did full stops and commas matter? What did nouns and verbs matter? What did proper sentences matter, so long as you could grasp the meaning of two half sentences? What, after all, is good English *for* – and whom does it benefit?

There is a pyramid of categories. At the top is that substantial minority of professionals – writers, journalists, lawyers, administrators, academics and so on – who need good English to make a living. It is as essential to them as physics to a scientist.

A far larger category – in commerce, the service industries, the white-collar end of manufacturing – will find a command of English useful, but it is secondary to their work skills, and their careers do not hang upon it. The sales rep who brings in large orders, after all, is not about to lose his commission on account of the dangling participles in his report.

Then we come to a class who are *required* to have some grasp of English – secretaries, typists, lower-rung civil servants, local government officers – as a job qualification. However, the standard demanded of them has gradually fallen – some would say nosedived – with the deterioration of English skills at this level. In this group we find probably the main perpetrators of the spread of sub-literacy, particularly in spelling and punctuation (although they may have been very good at creative writing).

Finally, we have a broad base of those with no especial vocational need of English except perhaps peripherally in the writing of signs and notices, filing returns, making out order sheets etc. Otherwise this group's requirement is mainly social or domestic – letter-writing, form-filling, notes to the milkman.

All this is to ignore, which it must not, all those on every level who, regardless of any vocational need, value the language for the pleasure to be got out of it – to some extent from writing it, in letters or diaries perhaps, but mainly from reading it. The better we understand English, the more satisfaction we get from reading it (and vice versa. No one can read Jane Austen for the first time without realizing that, as someone said, grammar is wit).

Aside from this recreational enrichment, however, it is evident that a command of

English becomes more necessary the more people use it in their work, and less necessary the less the workplace calls for it. So the question arises, then why should a good grounding in the language be regarded as an essential for all, regardless of utilitarian need?

The devil's advocate might echo, 'Why indeed?' We use language most in speech, and colloquial spoken English pays scant regard to formal rules. When even Royal personages may be heard in TV interviews saying *he and I* when they mean *him and me*, and a Prime Minister may describe inflation as *the worser of two evils*, it is clearly the consensus that fluency in speech is more important than grammar and structure. Then why, if nobody minds one way or the other whether we can punctuate or spell or construct a sentence, should we impose more stringent standards when it comes to the written word? Isn't fluency, or self-expression as we seem to prefer to call it when applied to the written word, still more important than structure?

There are several answers to that. The most obvious one is that bad English is far harder to read than to listen to. If you don't understand what someone has said, you can always ask for it to be repeated. If you don't understand what someone has written, you can only try to puzzle it·out. *I began to doubt that the murders could not be solved.* Does that mean they could be solved or they couldn't be solved?

In commercial terms, bad English is simply not cost-effective – which is not to say that good English may be left to those who can make a profit out of it. If we allow correct English to be but a specialist subject for those with a vocational use for it, then the upper reaches of the pyramid will always be denied to those on the lower slopes because they will not be equipped to climb it. No, the successful sales rep will not be fired for his faulty syntax – but will he be promoted?

Another practical consideration is that employers often demand a higher level of literacy than the job requires. Equating competence in simple English composition with intelligence, they especially look for literacy in job applications. And rightly so: the job applicant who can compose a well-written letter has a more organized mind than the one who can't – a useful work skill.

The wider answer is a social one. Bad English as daily encountered by all classes in every branch of their lives – the greengrocer's *banana's*, British Rail's chalked *regret's for delay's*, the audio-typist who doesn't know the difference between *principle* and *principal* (or between *there* and *their*, for that matter), the sub-literate junk mail, the newspaper peppered with grammatical errors and seemingly hellbent on establishing common acceptance of an apostrophe in the possessive *its* – is part of the general corrosion of the quality of life, like vandalism, litter and graffiti. Like these eyesores too, it proliferates:

the more slipshod English in circulation, the wider the assumption that it doesn't matter any more, that the Queen's English is by now the quaint preserve of pedants wearily objecting to the wrong use of *hopefully* for the nth time.

It shows how far down the slippery slope we have edged when you consider that no social stigma attaches to semi-literacy. Complete illiterates will confess that their motivation for attending remedial classes was a sense of shame at being unable to read; yet people from all walks of life will cheerfully admit, without embarrassment, that they are hopeless at spelling and punctuation, don't know enough grammar to cover a postage stamp and dread having to write letters. But it would be unjust, as well as unfruitful, to wish the illiterate's sense of shame on all those who, through inadequate teaching rather than inadequate attention to what was being taught, cannot put a sentence together. Far better to instil a sense of pride in those who can. The ability to express oneself in clear, correct English is an accomplishment, like being able to play the piano. Not everyone can do it well, but for sure everyone can learn how not to do it badly.

From Victorian times until the early postwar years, parents who wanted their children to make their way in the world were forever correcting their English and urging them to 'speak properly'. With increasingly sloppy usage on radio and television, not to mention their own uncertain grasp of the language, today's parents seem, on the face of it, to have given up the battle. Yet they still yearn for their children to be able to express themselves effectively; not only that, where they too have missed out on proper English lessons, they too long to be able to express themselves effectively.

So far as the up-and-coming generation is concerned, we are in the hands of the teachers who are in the hands of their administrators who are in the hands of the educational policy makers, advised by committees of the great and the good who have pondered deeply and at length on what children should know at certain stages of their education, and perhaps less deeply and at shorter length on what teachers should know in order to inform them.

Whether the next decade will see a turn-around in English teaching only time, and the standard of written job applications around the year 2000, will tell. Most likely, given the administrative chaos of the new national curriculum, there needs to be one more upheaval in the schools and teacher training colleges before anything like a reforming programme gets under way.

Meanwhile, what is to be done for all those lost legions of the language who, for three decades, have been leaving school without a proper grasp of English? They want a better understanding not only for themselves but in order to help their children, assuming classroom teaching remains imperfect. But where to turn? They can always go back to school, of course – night school, rather; but that means a regular commitment of time and in any case not everyone is keen to start again from scratch in a class of widely varying abilities. The only alternative, unless one is going to take on a private tutor, is self-help.

The problem here, however, is that when it comes to learning or re-learning at home, even the most basic books on English tend to assume some knowledge of grammar, which for those who barely know the difference between object and subject can make them as daunting as advanced computer manuals – for instance, *Where the subject is the source of action of the verb, then the verb is said to be in the active voice.* And here we catch the active voice of the latter-day English teacher, asking triumphantly whether this example does not prove what opponents of the naming of parts have been saying all along, namely that grammatical terminology taken out of context is confusing and unhelpful.

Up to a point. The flaw in this argument is its assumption that when it comes to knowing how the language is structured, the untutored mind is as a blank sheet of blotting paper, simply waiting to absorb. This is far from the truth. Discounting a substantial underclass of sub-literates, most people, whatever their standard of education or level of achievement, have a far surer command of the complexities of the English language than many of them realize (give or take a few blind spots).

They have had it from the earliest age. Children coming into kindergarten bring an amazing amount of knowledge with them, and it is all knowledge about language. Parents teaching their children counting-games – *one potato, two potato* and so on – may imagine that they are teaching the rudiments of arithmetic. So they are, but that is of minimal importance, since the child is going to learn to count anyway. What is important is that the child has learned how to express the concept of counting in English. Without that in-built knowledge which the child brings into school, the teacher can get nowhere. Even where parents have no awareness of having taught their children anything at all – there are sad cases of five year olds arriving at school without even a scrap of a nursery rhyme or skipping song to contribute – they have, consciously or not, taught them how to speak.

So children do not go to school to learn their language. They take their language to school in order to learn. Obviously, if they are being properly educated, they will learn more of, and about, the language as they go along – their vocabulary will improve, they will find more complex sentence constructions, and so on. But English is the only subject to which they come so well prepared and with such a wealth of prior knowledge. Imagine the first day of geometry in a mathematics class where before the teacher has even entered the room the pupils already know how to use a set-square, compasses and dividers and have a working knowledge of triangles and parallelograms. Imagine, to continue the analogy, that the teacher then refuses to impart the Pythagoras theorem on the grounds that it will be over their heads.

From the moment we are able to talk we begin to absorb hundreds of rules governing the language, but so effortlessly that we are hardly aware of the process. When, with the past tense *gave* not yet in its vocabulary, a toddler lisps, *I did give my sweets to Mary*, it is using the past tense of the auxiliary verb *to do* to vary the tense of the verb *to give* – a highly sophisticated means of remedying the deficiency. The same child, taking the present tense, might say, *I do be giving my sweets to Mary*, revealing an understanding not only of present participles but of the role of two auxiliary verbs in helping to express tense and voice respectively. Long before it learns to write, the child is displaying a grasp of syntax already so ingrained as to seem instinctive.

So this subliminal learning process goes on all through early life as our bank of knowledge of how the language works builds up. But having built up, it begins to silt up. Where in childhood we would have said with unthinking confidence, *These sweets are for you and me*, we now falter and wonder if it shouldn't be *These sweets are for you and I*. To anyone hazy on personal pronouns, *you and I* seems 'the done thing' – the grammatical equivalent of the crooked little finger when sipping tea. It doesn't actually *sound* correct – but in our uncertainty we refuse to listen to that inner voice we were instructed by when young.

Take *lay* and *lie* as another example. Most people know there is a difference between the two, but the distinction has grown fuzzy. We may vaguely recognize that *I laid on the grass* is wrong, yet not know why. The answer happens to be that the transitive verb *lay* cannot be used intransitively. But that is no use to the non-grammarian. Even if we are able to grasp that a transitive verb has a direct object while an intransitive verb doesn't, we cannot tell one from the other (or we think we can't), and even if we could it would not get us very far, since many transitive verbs may be used intransitively and vice versa.

Yet we reckon without that subliminal knowledge. Somewhere in the mists of memory is the knowledge that *laid* (as in *laid an egg*) is the past tense of *lay*, while *lay* (as in *I lay down*) is the past tense of *lie*. Many of us may also very well recall how confusion came to set in – with *Now I lay me down to sleep*, which makes archaic use of the transitive *lay* (*put to rest*) although it does happen to be correct. But perhaps we should have memorized *In a cowslip's bell I lie* instead. Notwithstanding, without recourse to any grammatical paraphernalia we know that *I laid on the grass* has something wrong with it.

It sounds as if I provided the grass, as in *I laid on the drinks*. The sentence needs tuning, and there is only one alternative note. *I lay on the grass* sounds right and is right.

Using the seemingly instinctive knowledge we have of how English works, augmented by a short crash course on some of the things we may have forgotten, we can develop a keen ear for the language by getting into the habit of monitoring the sound and the sense of the words we are using. This is not to say we are all about to become latter-day Hazlitts or Jane Austens. Nor does it even mean that we shall have a complete grasp of English grammar. Going back to those transitive and intransitive verbs, for example, *To sleep* is an intransitive verb, having no direct object. Less obviously, while it is not supposed to be used transitively, it sometimes is, as in *Our timeshare flat sleeps seven*. The head swims. But we do not have to concern ourselves with all these grammatical ins and outs. We recognize a colloquialism when we see one and so we know that *Our timeshare flat sleeps seven* is acceptable English.

Despite its infinite nuances and infuriating inconsistencies (*bough, cough* and all that), English is a straightforward enough language which foreigners (equipped, true enough, with the principles of grammar) find easy to learn. Grammar is thinking, said Iris Murdoch; and English responds well to logical analysis. Whoever framed the bank advertisement quoted earlier, *What's orange, got three legs and eats melons?*, must know perfectly well that *what's* is a contraction of *what is*, that there is an implied *has* before *got*, and that the *is* of *what's orange* cannot possibly supply the *has* of *has got*. Had he said *What's orange, has three legs* etc. he would have kept out of trouble; and that is doubtless what he meant to say, but he confused his *got* with his *has* and then failed to sound out this bit of nonsense for grammatical sense.

Again, if the speaker who said *Just because Brussels has made a decision, you cannot say that me as a farmer have got to follow it* had thought his statement through, he would have realized that he could not say *me have* (or *me has*, come to that). Even if he has never had a grammar lesson in his life he must know, when he thinks about it, that he should have said *that I as a farmer have got to follow it*.

You may not know that *Coming down the stairs, the light bulb fell out of its socket and landed at my feet* infringes the rule that a participial phrase at the opening of a sentence must refer to the subject. What you do know is that it was *I*, not *the light bulb*, that was coming down the stairs, and that the sentence had better read *As I was coming down the stairs* etc.

It takes a keener ear to spot what is wrong with *Five men are in hospital after a ship sank in the Humber*, which is that the two verbs – *are*, *sank* – should be in concord, that is to say they should agree in tense, number, gender and person. The problem is that *are*, from the verb *to be*, suggests a more permanent state of affairs – *God is good, we are adults* etc. – than is carried by the specific event *sank*. If we allow *after* to make the two verbs compatible, the sentence would read either *Five men were sent to hospital after a ship sank in the Humber* or *Five men are in hospital after the sinking of a ship in the Humber*.

Not all gaffes in English are grammatical errors: far from it. A reviewer in the *Spectator* reproved the Prime Minister for being ungrammatical in saying *Trial by television is the day that freedom dies*. A reader pointed out, rightly: 'It is not ungrammatical. It is, however, strictly speaking, complete nonsense – like, say, *Sneezing is 4ft 9in*.' Then there are errors of carelessness: *In this episode our born loser is in the farming business – but not the kind that includes furry creatures or our feathered friends. The only birds are two-legged ones*. (That piece of copy from the *TV Times* must have gone through a dozen pairs of hands without anyone querying *two-legged* birds.) There is English that reads as if it had been composed with a poker: *The classroom is the learning environment where interaction occurs between teachers and learners*. There is jargon and there is gobbledygook (sometimes spelled gobbledegook) and there is shoddy English and there is overblown English, and there is English so confused or obscure that it might as well be Welsh. All can be remedied.

Common sense tells us that *civil engineer* does not need a hyphen since there is no possibility of mistaking him for an engineer who has found that it pays to be polite. Our sense of symmetry tells us that *two years' imprisonment* needs an apostrophe because of the precedent set by *one year's imprisonment*. Our sense of the absurd tells us that *Outside, it was raining* is a pretty fatuous thing to say, since the likelihood of it raining inside is remote. The ear tells us that *For who the bell tolls* is a misquotation. Anyone capable of rational thought, however ill-educated, could without difficulty build up, from hundreds, thousands, of similar examples, an impressive dictionary of what we already know, what we have somehow picked up as we have gone along, about the English language. And so while this manual does not set itself up as a course in English Without Tears, anyone able to read it without difficulty is already half way towards developing, and in time perfecting, a facility for writing in clear, expressive English.

The purpose of language is to say what we mean (though not necessarily to mean what we say), and the purpose of grammar is to help us say it. How much grammar you need depends upon how much knowledge about language you need. To return to the linguists' car analogy: some drivers do indeed want to know about the workings of the internal combustion engine: it saves them a fortune in garage bills. Others are content to join the AA.

Grammarians are fond of quoting a snatch

from *Macbeth*: '. . . No; this my hand will rather/ The multitudinous seas incarnadine,/ Making the green one red', and then challenging one on how to read *green one red*. Their solution is that you have to understand that *incarnadine* is a transitive verb, that the *multitudinous seas* is its object, and that *one* functions as an adjunct rather than as a pronoun, so that *green* is a noun while *red* may be either a noun or, more likely, an adjective. Most people are not equipped to play such games. They are capable, however, upon hearing those lines spoken by a competent Shakespearian actor, of at least following their drift, if not of positively understanding them. This book is for that audience.

Part One

The Words. . .

Give Us the Tools

Any competent specialist in the English language could quickly run up a list of upwards of two thousand linguistic terms – *linguistics* being itself a linguistic term meaning the study of language.

Happily only a few hundred people in the whole country need to know words like *homonym, monoptote, enclitic*. For the rest of us, wanting only to be competent in English, a mere handful of terms will suffice, and they are all relatively simple.

If we are to understand what a sentence can and cannot do, we have to know about sentence construction and the parts of speech that go into it, and we have to know about punctuation. We ought to be able to clear up some of the confusions that frequently arise in English such as the difference between *which* and *that*. Finally, in an age when colloquial English is acceptable to a greater or lesser degree in all but the most formal writing, we ought to have some idea of what we can get away with.

This section is not a crash course in grammar, it is a crash course in the use of English, with strict grammatical limitations. For instance, it does not set out to explain in lay language that a relative clause is a secondary clause joined to an antecedent, since we all know a relative clause when we see one and don't necessarily need to know it by name. It does explain what a misrelated participle is when it is at home, because a misrelated participle can do the same damage to a sentence as a weevil to a biscuit.

However, technical terms are kept to a minimum and are explained as we go along.

Sentence

This is a sentence: *That's that*. This is another, from Thomas Hardy: *Occasionally, when the miller was bolting there was added to these continuous sounds the cheerful clicking of the hopper, which did not deprive them of rest except when it was kept going all night; and over and above all this they had the pleasure of knowing that there crept in through every crevice, door, and window of their dwelling, however tightly closed, a subtle mist of superfine flour from the grinding room, quite invisible, but making its presence known in the course of time by giving a pallid and ghostly look to the best furniture.*

In other words, a sentence can be pretty well what you want it to be. Traditional grammarians insist upon, at minimum, a subject and a verb, the *subject* being the noun which performs the action of the main verb: in *I am*, the subject is *I* and *am* the verb. They would much prefer it if the sentence had an object too. The object is the person or thing to which the verb is directed: in *I love you*, *I* is the subject, *love* the verb and *you* the object, not only of the subject's desires but of the sentence. But not only do many sentences not have an object, they frequently don't have verbs either, for example *Not so. Of course. Definitely.* Those grammarians will quibble that there is always a verb implied: *That is not so. Of course it is. It definitely is.* But they will not better one of the *OED*'s definitions of a sentence, which is *Such a portion of composition or utterance as extends from one full stop to another.* While this fails to define the first sentence of any piece of writing, it should serve us.

But while a sentence can be what you want it to be, it cannot be just what you please. Even bereft of its grammatical credentials, it has to follow grammatical rules. For example you cannot write *What brings a place alive are the people who live there*, because if you could, you might equally well write *What bring a place alive is the people who lives there*, which would be absurd.

Errors of this kind are dealt with under their appropriate headings below. There are other traps, not all of them grammatical in nature, into which an unthinking sentence might fall.

One is when the sentence is not a sentence at all. You may write *All right* and call it a sentence. *All right, let's go* is a sentence still, and so is *All right, let's go and see*; but you cannot write *All right, let's go and see whether* and put a full stop after it in the belief that it is a sentence, because that *whether* has opened up another clause which demands to be completed. A sentence can do without practically any ingredient except what is patently missing from it.

Another example of the incomplete sentence is the sentence chopped in two. It is all right, in the proper context, if done for narrative effect: *He threw open the door. No one there*. In the wrong context, the split sentence gives the reader an unintentional jolt: *She saw him only once again, by chance. In the elevator of a department store*. If the elevator has dramatic significance, then the full stop is justified, otherwise it should be a comma. The reason it isn't is that the writer probably thought, wrongly, that *by chance* would sit too awkwardly in the middle of a sentence.

A sentence has to be an entity. While you may link two sentences with a conjunction (*and, but, because* etc.) or a semicolon, they have to be closely connected. *The clock struck four; Mary filled the kettle* is one sentence, since it is the clock reaching teatime that presumably moves Mary to fill the kettle. *The clock had stopped; Mary filled the kettle* is two sentences masquerading as one, since here the clock has nothing to do with the kettle. (See also 'The Spoken Comma'.)

But however closely connected, and however immaculately linked, fused sentences will fail if they degenerate into verbiage: *After the war the company returned to commercial printing, although it was not until 1949, with the availability of better equipment, that the production of technical books was re-introduced, when format standardization enabled good quality books to be produced at a low price, and for almost thirty years the price remained unchanged, with the catalogue of standard titles gradually increasing.* Grammatically the sentence could scarcely be faulted – yet, log-jammed by its seemingly endless succession of loosely connecting clauses, it is claustrophobically dreary, like a lapel-grabbing bore at a party who simply will not stop talking. The whole passage needs to be broken up: *After the war the company returned to commercial printing. However, it was not until 1949, with the availability of better equipment, that the production of technical books was re-introduced. Format standardization then enabled good quality books to be produced at a low price.* [Better as *With format standardization, good quality books could then be produced at a low price.*] *For almost thirty years, the price remained unchanged, with the catalogue of standard titles gradually increasing.*

It is not always necessary for a sentence to spell out every word. As often as not, words are omitted because they are implied, a process known as *ellipsis*. Most of these omissions are unconscious: the child who says *I have more seashells than you* is not aware of contracting the claim from *I have more seashells than you have seashells*. The language is shot through with accepted ellipses, most of which will bear analysis. *I have no objection: do you?* may look as if the two verbs *have* and *do* don't match, but what the second half of the sentence is really saying is *do you* have *any objection?* In *The thief was caught and his booty confiscated* there is an implied *was* before *confiscated*. In *The thief was caught, his booty confiscated, his possessions seized*, there are now implied two *ands*, a *was* and a *were*. *It depends who's paying* includes an implied *upon*. The most ungrammatical of non-grammarians, having got the knack of it, could produce examples without number.

Yet we are not entitled to drop words out of sentences at the drop of a hat. *False ellipsis* is where words have been left out that had better been left in, often with disastrous results. *The Vicar came all the way from St Mary's for tea, the odd job man to mend the vacuum cleaner, and the gardener his wages* has the odd job man coming all the way from St Mary's and the gardener mending his wages.

The further away the excised words from what they match, the less likely is the sentence to work: *He chose the steak, and his wife, who was going through one of her vegetarian phases when she could not abide anything cooked, the salad* may leave the reader wondering what *the salad* is doing there. Note that in any case we should not write *He chose the steak, but his wife the salad*, because some conjunctions – for example *but, because, after, though* – often take less kindly to ellipses than others. Go by the sound. *She was a vegetarian but* (she was) *not a fanatical one* is all right, but we would never write, it is to be hoped, *She chose the salad, because a vegetarian.*

Sentences whose verbs change voice – that is, from the active to the passive or vice versa (see *Verb* below) – likewise resist ellipses. *I do not think I can do the work in time, although I could if I had some help* cuts out *do it* after *could*, which is perfectly acceptable. *I do not think I can do the work in time, although it could be if help were provided* changes voice and so must not lose the *done* after *be*. On the other hand, in sentences which change from plural to singular or the other way round, ellipses are in order: *They are going, I* (am) *not; One was hanged, twelve* (were) *reprieved.*

That is a much-omitted little word. *I dreamt that I dwelt in marble halls* could just as easily read *I dreamt I dwelt. . . The girl that I marry* may be *The girl I marry.* But do not make the common journalistic mistake of over-omission. *I understand that you wished to see me and that you have complained that I refused to make an appointment* could profitably lose its first *that;* but *I understand you wished to see me and you have complained I refused to make an appointment* is muddling. As for *She and her Cabinet know perfectly well the fact they are rarely seen at any opera will make no difference to the next election*, the writer has omitted his *thats* to make a cumbersome passage less cumbersome, yet has succeeded only in making it more so.

Where a verb is to be implied in a list, it has to be established in the first item, not in the middle. *Until motorists drive better, motorcyclists learn left from right and cyclists how to pedal, we will have death on our roads* will not do. There has to be unity – which could have been supplied with *Until motorists learn how to drive better, motorcyclists how to tell left from right, and cyclists how to pedal. . .*

Leaving ellipses behind, parts of a sentence parallel in meaning should be harmonious in form. *His function was to look for errors, and their correction* is switching styles in mid-sentence. Read *His function was to look for errors and to correct them*. Items in a list should match in style. For *He stressed that opening hours would stay the same, no staff cuts, and a review of the training scheme*, read *He stressed that opening hours would stay the same, that there would be no staff cuts, and that there would be a review of the training scheme*.

Make sure that every sentence has its words in the right order. *He nearly walked two miles* is not the same as *He walked nearly two miles*. Words that modify the action, as *nearly* does, should go where they cannot be misunderstood.

Sentences that make fools of themselves are common. *For those of you who tuned in earlier, you'll have realized that we've been having technical problems* starts one sentence but finishes another. *Those of you who tuned in earlier will have realized* etc. is what the sentence has to say; it is difficult to work out where *For those of you who tuned in* intended to go before it encountered technical problems. *Male colleagues probably feel that, being women, it is their duty to protect female colleagues* is to sentence construction what the old Irish joke is to the question of how to get to Tipperary: 'If I were you, I wouldn't set off from here.'

Sentences going awry because of misdirected participles are discussed under *Verb* below. For the time being, two things remain to be said. Any sentence that has to be re-read is a bad sentence. And sheer carelessness can scupper a sentence even when it has charted a safe course through syntax. *Nudity, four-letter words and so on are now commonplace on radio and TV . . . There is an irreversible trend towards freedom and democracy in Europe; but this may change . . . I don't want to make the wrong mistake . . .* Check everything for sense.

Verb

Some of us were taught at school that a verb is *a doing word*, a definition some teachers jib at and others jeer at. Certainly it is difficult to say what is being done in a statement like *I like coffee* – or is it? The verb *to like* asserts the action of the subject, and the action of the subject is that he is sitting there liking coffee. In *I sat and watched the grass grow*, three verbs are called into play to describe what is going on, for all that it is very little.

Yet if a verb is a doing word, a doing word is not necessarily a verb in the popularly understood sense. When Shakespeare in his advice to the players says of an overblown performance that 'it out-herods Herod', he is taking a noun, and a proper noun at that, and turning it into the verb *to herod*. So a word does not necessarily need the pedigree of conjugation (*I herod, you herod* etc.) to qualify as a verb (see *Noun* below).

Conjugating verbs, selecting the correct form for every possible tense, mood, voice etc. – *I do, you do, he does* . . . all the way to *I am doing, I was doing, I should be doing* and so on – is something most of us do instinctively and usually correctly, although some of the finer points once learned in grammar schools such as *thou dost* and *thou wilt do* may elude us. This goes for regular and irregular verbs alike. A child, while not knowing what a past participle is, will know that the past participle of *sing* is *sung*, and so may at first conclude, with admirable logic, that the past participle of *bring* is *brung*, with the added possibility of the past tense *brang*. Pretty soon it will add *brought* to its vocabulary, and thereafter will never forget it. So only one fragment of the conjugation table need trouble us here, and that is where the verb ends in *-ing*.

We come at once to the bothersome *un-attached participle*. A present participle is that part of a verb ending in *-ing* where it is used as an adjective – *shopping (shopping trolley)*, *walking (walking shoes)*. (Where it is a noun – as in *I hate walking* – it is called a *gerund*. That need not detain us here.) A *participle phrase* is an adjective phrase – *Walking down the street one day* – which attaches itself to the subject: *Walking down the street one day, he saw a dog*. The trouble is that very often it does no such thing, and we get sentences like this: *Walking down the street one day, a dog crossed his path* – and so suddenly it is the dog which is walking down the street, and not the man.

There we have an unattached participle. To repeat: where it functions as an adjective the participle phrase must refer directly to the subject. We cannot even have *Walking down the street one day, his path was crossed by a dog*, since *he* is the subject, not *his path*, although some non-purists would argue that *he* is implied in *his path*. Really, we should have something on the lines of *Walking down the street one day, he came across a dog*. (The dog will have to cross his path, if that is necessary to the plot, in the next sentence.)

There are far sillier examples of wandering participles at large in everyday print. *Being in need of a paint job, I got £200 knocked off the list price*. I am not in need of a paint job, the car is. Then we have the participle phrase that forgets its own existence: *Writing in the current Spectator, the novelist A.N. Wilson, once the original Young Fogie, writes in most disrespectful tones about the Royal Family*. Boiled down, this is *Writing in the Spectator, A.N. Wilson writes*, which is brazen repetition.

There has to be a substitute for *writes. . . about*: *refers . . . to* will do nicely.

Other possible problems with verbs are relatively straightforward:

• A verb must agree with its subject: that is, a singular noun dèmands a singular verb (*A whole range of goods is available*, not *are available*) and a plural noun a plural verb (*The goods you ordered from our range are available*). In *The kind of activity we are able to provide – bridge, chess, Scrabble etc. – are much appreciated by the residents*, the second *are* refers to *activity*, not to the intervening bundle of activities. We would not say *The kind of activity we can provide are*, so the *are* must be *is*.

• The same goes for linking verbs. *One service the council provides are the thousands of metal notices which publicize its good deeds*. Here *provides* is right, but *are* is not, since that too refers back to *one service* (subject) as well as forward to *metal notices* (object). Allow the sentence to keep its nerve.

• *I'm Jack Smith and among other members of the reporting team we've been looking at how local government works*. No: the *we've* has to be *I've*. If you start in the first person singular you cannot then switch to the first person plural just because you have picked up a few people on the way.

• One verb dependent upon another must agree with it in tense. *How would I be affected if I can't pay?* should be either *How would I be affected if I couldn't pay?* or *How will I be affected if I can't pay?* Exception: since the present tense may be used for the future, it is in order to say *We go to the country tomorrow, when we shall meet up with Uncle Charlie.*

Certain words create confusion as to whether they call for singular or plural verbs. These are the main troublemakers:

• *Either* and *neither* take a singular verb. *Either she or he was there*, not *were there*. *Neither of them was in*, not *were in*.

• But in *neither/nor*, the verb agrees with the nearest subject. *Neither he nor they were there. Neither they nor he was there.*

• Two singular nouns connected with *or* take a singular verb. *He or she was to be there.*

• *Both* is plural: *Both were there.*

• *With* is singular: *The Queen, with her lady-in-waiting, was in the parlour.*

• *Each*, as the subject, is singular. *Each boy has an apple.* Where a plural noun is the subject, *each* takes a plural too. *The boys each have an apple.*

• *Every* is singular. *Every bar, restaurant and café was open.*

• *Everyone, someone, everybody, nobody,* all take a singular verb; but only a pedant would object to granting them a plural personal pronoun: *Everyone in the school loves their headmaster* may be illogical, but *Everyone in the school loves his or her headmaster* is ludicrous. (A better alternative would have been *the headmaster.*)

• *One of* is singular or plural, according to the sense. *One of the finest aircraft which have ever flown. One of our aircraft is missing. One of the funniest comedies there have ever been. One of my comedies is to be played on Broadway.*

Items in a list take a plural verb, alternatives in a list the singular: *A cat, a dog and a canary were her chosen pets*; but *A cat, a dog or a canary is her choice of pet.*

Finally, verbs have their voices – the *active voice* and the *passive voice*. *I love you* is the active voice, *You are loved by me* the passive voice. There are occasions (this is one of them) when for one reason or another it is difficult to avoid the unloved passive voice, indeed where it may be preferable; but the active should always be favoured where possible. Even more to be cold-shouldered is the *impersonal passive voice* usually encountered in reports and business correspondence: *It is believed . . . One is given to understand . . . It is to be hoped that . . .* Who believes? Who is given to understand? Who hopes? The impersonal passive voice is usually a deliberate choice, enabling the writer to hide behind his official mask. Some institutions still discourage their staff from writing in the first person, in the belief that the active voice encourages chattiness and over-familiarity. If HM Inspector of Taxes can write in the first person, so can most of his clients.

Noun

In *red roses*, the word *red* is an adjective. In *dressed in red*, it is a noun. But if we are not to go into the grammatical complexities we may content ourselves with saying that a noun is a thing, place, person or quality. The first three categories are concrete – *geranium, Birmingham, Uncle Charlie*. The other is abstract – *happiness, skill, fear, laughter*.

The first thing to be said about nouns is that abstract nouns should be used sparingly, and always be tethered firmly to concrete nouns. Abstract nouns may well express powerful ideas and emotions, but without constant reference to the real world in which they exist, they can be very heavy going: *Note, however, that consciousness is not a passive state, but a phase of activity, the doing of something in the face of a situation, and it implies the quality of being aware and responding to the situation. Thus the consciousness of the situation does not consist simply in perceiving in a static sense what is there present, but in perceiving, estimating, anticipating the outcome of present change.* Sixteen nouns and pronouns and not a person or a tangible thing in sight.

Lincoln's Gettysburg Address, by contrast, dramatically expresses an abstract philosophy by constantly referring back to the people to whom it applies. Consider the clever juxtaposition of concrete and abstract nouns (pronouns omitted) tabulated below.

CONCRETE	ABSTRACT
	years
fathers	
continent	

CONCRETE	ABSTRACT
	nation
	liberty
	proposition
men	
	war
	nation
	any nation
	(hypothetical)
battlefield	
	war
field	
resting place	
	lives
	nation
	sense
ground	
men	
	power
world	
the living	
	work
	task
the dead	
	devotion
	cause
	measure
	devotion
the dead	
	nation
	God
	birth
	freedom
	government

CONCRETE	ABSTRACT
the people	
the people	
the people	
the earth	

They are all simple, striking nouns; but those twenty-three abstract nouns need the sixteen concrete nouns that buttress them to help them express what they have to say in terms that anyone can understand and identify with.

But we are straying into ground covered in Part Two. Let us move on to some other points to be made about nouns.

Where the root of an abstract noun is a verb, it is a good idea where possible to ditch the noun and go back to the verb form, so that *if the possibility exists* becomes *if possible*, and *use verbs in preference to abstract nouns* becomes *prefer verbs to abstract nouns*.

The noun as verb – *fax, telephone* – exercises some people strangely. In fairness they will allow Shakespeare's *out-herods*: their fury is usually directed at the jargon noun-verb as in *We will resource your order from another branch*. They have a point. *Input*, not a pretty word, becomes even less pretty when turned into a verb: *inputted*. On the other hand, newly minted noun-verbs are often very colourful, for example *to handbag* which enjoyed a vogue in political circles for some months. Resist making verb extensions out of nouns which have a verb already. The verb of

19

implementation is *implement*, not *implementationalize*. That way madness lies, and *implementation* becomes *implementationalization*. Resist even more the verb invented out of a noun. *Anonym* and *anonymity* are nouns, *anonymous* and *anonymal* (rare) adjectives, and that is about as far as that word has to go. *Anonymize* (used by the Department of Health) is an ersatz verb, and an awkward one.

Nouns very often double as adjectives, when they are called *modifiers*: *health shop*, *peace talks*, *pencil sharpener*. Sometimes they more than double: *emergency deployment readiness exercise* – a tendency firmly to be avoided. Go by usage whether you fuse a modifier or not: *bathroom*, *bathmat*, *bathrobe*, but *bath plug*. Do not put a noun serving as an adjective into adjectival form: *drama class*, *education studies*, not *dramatic class*, *educational studies*. Modifiers are always singular: *drug smuggler*, not *drugs smuggler*.

The idea of pronouns – *he, she, it, who, which, my, you, his, this, that, each, either, some* etc. – is to give the noun represented a rest, so that we are not writing sentences like *John picked up John's book and opened the book where John had marked the book when John had last read the book*. But a pronoun must not be admitted until the noun it stands in for – its *antecedent*, as it is called – has been identified. In *He applied for membership but it was turned down*, the pronoun applies not to *membership* but to *his application*, which is not present in the sentence.

Keep pronouns simple – *I, me, you, him*, not *myself, yourself, himself* – unless the idea is to stress the person involved. *Yourself, John, Mary and myself* is unnecessary: what is wrong with *You, John, Mary and I*? But *The Minister himself will be there*, to indicate that he will be coming in person, is justifiable.

Be careful when using the same pronoun for two different things in proximity: *He gave the dog its dinner. It looked disgusting*. The dog or the dinner? Then there is the old chestnut much loved by grammarians: *If the baby does not thrive on fresh milk, boil it*. Where two or more people of the same sex inhabit a sentence, it is prudent to bestow pronouns on only one of them, to avoid situations like *John went to see Uncle Charlie to tell him that he was not now eligible for membership, but that he would take it up with the committee*. We are at a loss: which of the pair is not now eligible for membership? We could write . . . *to tell him that he (Uncle Charlie) was not now eligible for membership, but that he (John) would take it up with the committee*. We could call Uncle Charlie *the latter* and John *the former*, but that would give us a stiff-necked sentence. Pronoun-strewn sentences are often better recast altogether, but if we are to stick to this form it had better be *John went to see Uncle Charlie to tell him that he was not now eligible for membership; but that John would take it up with the committee*.

Some notes on plural and singular:

• Collective nouns may be singular or plural. You can say *the Government is* or *the*

Government are. What you cannot say is *The Government is considering whether to revise their poll tax legislation*; you have to stay with the singular or plural. As to which it should be in the first place, go by the sense. *The Government is debating* should be *The Government are debating*, since one body cannot debate with itself; but *The Government is the only institution to refer to its members by place names*, because one institution is one thing. *The public are not fools* and *The public is not fooled* are equally acceptable.

• A singular noun may be used with a plural possessive. *That was how they earned their living. They held their breath.* But: *That was how they performed their tasks. They held their drinks.* The singular noun – *living, breath* – is common to *they*, while the plural – *tasks, drinks* – is a number of things identified with separate individuals.

• Nouns connected by *and* usually take a plural verb. In *The Minister's vacillation and procrastination has lost the confidence of the public*, the *has* should be *have*. But: *The top and bottom of it is that fish and chips is my favourite dish*. Go by what rings true.

• Plural nouns whose meaning is singular take a singular verb: *Measles is catching. Criteria, data, media* are all plural nouns requiring plural verbs. *Stadiums* now seem to be edging *stadia* out of the language.

• Whether plural or singular, proper nouns – names of people, countries, institutions, etc. – are entitled to capital initial letters. Common nouns are not: but they are sometimes honoured above their station. *The Government* is a proper noun. In *The art of government* it is not. *The Cabinet* may take a capital (some newspapers don't bother), but *He will be asked to form a Cabinet* is wrong, because the cabinet in question does not yet exist.

Common nouns are occasionally given capital letters for facetious effect: *He was a Very Important Person. We were solemnly assured that we had Never Had It So Good.* The device smacks of *Punch* in the 1930s, and a very little of it goes a long way.

Adjective

Adjectives come in three categories: those derived from nouns (*beautiful, fortunate, liverish*), those derived from verbs (*haunting, chatty, willing*), and those which appear to exist in their own right, although they may well have antecedents lost in history (*happy, bland, high*). In all three categories appear words which some may be surprised to hear are adjectives at all: *three, this, many, her.* This is because adjectives are far more than 'describing words', to use yet another expression despised by teachers; they are also defining words, with many functions. Their chief one, true enough, is to describe, or qualify: *a beautiful day, a willing accomplice, a red dress.* But to speak of *that person there* is to use an adjective. All numbers are adjectives, where they are not used as nouns as in *a cool million. My, his, your*, expressing possession, are adjectives. *Seventh, nearest, inner*, expressing order or distance, are adjectives.

The adjective's near relation is the *adverb*, a word which modifies or qualifies a verb, an adjective, another adverb, or even a whole sentence, mainly by adding *-ly* to an adjective: *abjectly, happily, possibly*. Words like *now, then, before, after*, which answer the question *when?*; words like *here, there, near*, which answer the question *where?*; and words like *very, nearly, more*, which answer the question *how much?* are also adverbs. (Note that many words serve both as adverbs and adjectives, for example *very*. Among other definitions, *very* the adverb can mean *in a high degree*, as in *very happy*, while *very* the adjective can mean *absolute*, as in *the very end*.)

So the job of adjectives and adverbs is something more than to colour other words. It is, however, as a colouring agent that the adjective in particular is most mishandled. Inexperienced writers are inclined to lay on their adjectives with a trowel, like adolescent girls experimenting with make-up. *The dark green leaves of the richly verdant peace lilies glistened with fresh, sparkling, morning dew.* Given that most of us know the usual colour of leaves, this could be pruned to *the leaves of the peace lilies glistened with dew* with no loss to the reader at all. The first function of all adjectives is to inform, and none of the adjectives sprayed into that sentence tells us anything we don't know already, except perhaps that the author is seemingly unaware that *green* and *verdant* are the same thing.

Every adjective should earn its place. If it is there simply for effect, then it must be effectual. Study the masters of style and you will see how economical they are with their adjectives. The Bible, for example, never uses an adjective which could just as well be left out. Where it does allow in adjectives, they each have a point to make. *These six things doth the Lord hate . . . A proud look, a lying tongue, and hands that shed innocent blood, An heart that deviseth wicked imaginations, feet that be swift in running to mischief, A false witness that speaketh lies, and he that soweth discord among brethren.* Not one of the half dozen adjectives in that passage from Proverbs could be removed without doing harm to the text.

Avoid abstract adjectives where possible, especially lazy ones like *handsome, vivacious, jolly, stupendous, expensive*, which leave the reader to do the work. A *striking woman*: in what way does she strike? The author does not say, and so the reader has to picture her striking qualities for himself. *Blue and yellow, ten-ton, six foot three* are pieces of information. *Brightly coloured, heavy, tall* merely raise questions. Which colours? How heavy? How tall? So with abstract adverbs supposedly qualifying abstract adjectives: *relatively small* (relative to what?), *substantially true* (how true?), *comparatively few* (comparative with what?). How can the abstract qualify the abstract?

Shun adjectives and adverbs that qualify to

no purpose: *rather, quite, just, completely, absolutely*. We have seen instances of the use of *very*, and *very good* is generally accepted as being between *good* and *excellent*; but how rich is *very rich*, how poor *very poor*, and how cold *very cold*?

Do not use limpet adjectives. Some nouns find it almost impossible to get into print without being clamped to an unnecessary adjective: *Full inquiry, thorough investigation, drastic steps, real danger, paramount importance, mindless violence, utmost urgency, true facts*. Where the adjective merely echoes the noun, as in *grateful thanks* which might just as well be *thankful thanks*, cut it out.

This brings us to needless repetition, or *tautology*, of which there are examples without number. *Damp puddle, pre-arranged venue, mobile van, biggest majority, in actual fact, tall skyscraper, mutual agreement, strange phenomenon* all repeat adjectivally what their nouns have already said. *First* is a first-class source of tautology: *first invented, first initiated, first became, first discovered. First* is all right in *when we first met* (distinguishable from *when we last met*) and in *when we were first married*, meaning *when we first* (or *originally*) *were married*; but it should never be used before any word which is a first in its own right, as are all the above examples.

While they are certainly the ringleaders, adjectives and adverbs are by no means the only culprits in the spread of tautology and its twin *pleonasm* (using more words than necessary, as in *I am keenly looking forward with great eagerness*). Verbs and nouns are all too capable of combining to say the same thing twice (*razed to the ground, sang a song, fashioned a creation*), while nouns need little encouragement to do it on their own (*husband-and-wife couple, strike action, pair of twins*). They also take a good share of the blame for other forms of tautology: unnecessary elaboration (*the prison's captive population*), superfluous description (*white snow*), needless appendage (*weather situation*) and self-cancelling proposition (*We will either win or lose*).

All these solecisms may be avoided by checking each word's credentials before admitting it to a sentence. Is its journey really necessary, or has it turned up merely to duplicate the task of a word already in position? That said, it is true that repetition may sometimes be used for effect or emphasis, as in *I saw it with my own eyes*. *A single red rose* is technically tautology, but *a red rose* on its own would not have brought out its singularity.

Two final observations on adjectives and adverbs in general. An adjective turned into a noun is better off turned back into an adjective or adverb. *Probably* is better than *in all probability, it is possible that* better than *there is a possibility that, responsible for* better than *with responsibility towards*. An abstract noun accompanied by an adjective can often be slimmed down to a simple adjective or adverb, discarding the lifeless noun: *of a serious nature* becomes *serious*; *in a dilapidated condition* becomes *dilapidated*; *on a temporary basis* becomes *temporarily*.

Comparative (*small*, *smaller*) and superlative (*smallest*) adjectives take the *-er*, *-est* form where they are one syllable, or two syllables ending in *-y*: *big*, *bigger*, *biggest*; *silly*, *sillier*, *silliest*. Longer formations take *more* or *most*: *ridiculous*, *more ridiculous*, *most ridiculous*. some two-syllable words can take either *-er* and *-est* or *more* and *most*: *simple*, *simpler*, *simplest*; *more simple*, *most simple*. If in doubt, check with the dictionary. All adverbs which have the same form as adjectives take the same comparative and superlative form (*hard*, *harder*, *hardest*).

The one thing to remember about superlatives is that like a royal flush at poker they cannot be improved upon and so you cannot say *most silliest* (although you can say *much sillier* or *far more ridiculous*). The same goes for words indicating absolute quantities: stores may advertise dresses for the fuller figure but a thing cannot be *more full* or *most full*, and certainly not *more fuller*, although it may conceivably be *over-full*. Since a thing is either full or it is not full, *to the fullest extent* could be wrong, but usage allows it. *More empty* does not make sense – try *less crowded*. Some words are what may be termed incomparatives: *perfect*, *infinite*, *complete*, *impossible* cannot be improved upon; and we all know, although some of us forget, that nothing can be *quite unique*.

The Spoken Comma

Many years ago there was a wireless comedian known as Stainless Stephen whose act depended on spoken punctuation marks: 'And the weather exclamation mark! Do you know comma, it was raining cats and dogs semicolon'; and so on.

While no one goes to such lengths we do all use punctuation marks in our speech, indicated by pauses and inflections. When someone is talking to us, we unconsciously listen for the commas, colons and other stops that help the words make sense: 'Nearly all the family were there (*colon pause*): my mother (*comma pause*), my father (*comma pause*), two of my brothers (*dash pause and parenthetical inflection*) – not my eldest brother (*comma pause*), he couldn't make it (*dash pause*) – and who else (*interrogatory inflection*)? Oh (*comma pause*), yes (*colon pause*): Uncle Charlie (*terminal inflection, full stop pause*).

Since we learn to punctuate before we can write, it is odd that stops, usually commas, should present so much difficulty. It is not as if punctuation followed a rigid set of rules. In the four centuries or so that commas and full stops have been in common use (most other punctuation marks are even more recent), their terms of reference have changed many times over, mostly towards streamlining and simplification.

Stops do have a purely grammatical use. The full stop has the obvious task of marking the end of a sentence, the semicolon of marking the end of what might be called a subsentence. The comma has the important job of, to quote Fowler, 'separating inseparables' – a verb from its subject or object – or of distinguishing between those clauses introduced by *who* or *which* – known as a *defining relative clause* – and a *non-defining relative clause*. The defining relative does not take commas: *My wife who is in America is suing for maintenance* says that I have two or more wives, and one of them is in America where she is suing for maintenance. The nondefining relative is marked by commas: *My wife, who is in America, is suing for maintenance* admits to only one wife, who happens to be in America.

But there is really only one constant rule in punctuation, and that is that we must listen to what we are writing. Most misjudgements of punctuation occur because the writer is not playing his words back.

Next to any other car in its price range, the Fiat Croma looks expensive. In fact, it looks and per-

forms, a good six or seven thousand pounds better than it actually costs . . . No one would ever speak that second sentence as it is punctuated. We should either say *In fact it looks and performs a good six or seven thousand* etc. or *In fact it looks, and performs, a good six or seven thousand.* . . Both versions are acceptable – the former more so because it is the less fussy.

To write *Her first book about a mass murderer is to be made into a film* is to suggest the existence of several books about mass murderers, of which this is the first. In speech, given that we had to stick to the same words, we should automatically put in the pauses: *Her first book, about a mass murderer, is to be made into a film.*

That is an example where an absence of commas made a sentence ambiguous. In general, we are right to punctuate far less than we did. Two hundred years ago, Gibbon felt the need for no fewer than four commas and two semicolons in this not very long sentence: *The various modes of worship, which prevailed in the Roman world, were all considered by the people as equally true; by the philosopher, as equally false; and by the magistrate, as equally useful.* Today, with perhaps some loss of elegance yet no loss of clarity, we should probably make do with no more than two commas: *The various modes of worship which prevailed in the Roman world were all considered by the people as equally true, by the philosopher as equally false, and by the magistrate as equally useful.*

31

This is not to say that punctuation is to be regarded as a dying art. Stops – comma, semicolon, colon, full stop etc. – have an essential job to do. Indeed, they have two jobs: the functional one of making meaning clear, and the cosmetic one of enhancing style. This section looks at their functional role.

Comma
This is the most troublesome of all the stops, and it is never more so than when a sentence needs a pair of parenthetical commas to mark off a clause, word or phrase.

All too often, they are missed out altogether as in the *mass murderer* example quoted above; or as in *The toads are in danger because they have to cross the road on which people drive much too fast to get to their breeding grounds*, where the omission of the commas required after *road* and before *fast* may have been inspired by the author's realization that it would be an even more badly constructed sentence with stops than without them.

Even more commonly, only one comma is delivered where two are called for. *The Football League, which refused to heed three appeals to change the date of the match yesterday admitted its mistake*. The missing comma after *match* opens up the fleeting possibility that it was *yesterday* when the League refused to heed the appeals.

The Mayor considered calling for a ban on seaside holiday fixtures but has decided, at present not to. This is not so confusing, but it had better be either *but has decided at present not to* or *but has decided, at present, not to*.

Occasionally the second or closing comma may be implied. *He was the first, some said the only dramatist of that era* could stand a comma after *only*, but the *only* without a comma carries the sentence on where a comma would impede it. There is not a moment's reader puzzlement: that's the test.

That kind of exception apart, parenthetical commas should be regarded as on a par with brackets. Only an absent-minded writer would open a pair of brackets without ever closing it again. So it should be with pairs of commas.

The other great problem with commas is their under-use or over-use in going about their routine tasks.

A sentence which is effectively two sentences linked by a conjunction (*and, but, for, if, when* and other joining words) usually takes a comma before the conjunction. *They were all in good time for the conference, but the chairman was late for the reception.* But where there isn't a second subject (*the chairman*) or where the first subject (*they*) is implied in the other half of the sentence, no comma is necessary. *The chairman was in good time for the conference but late for the reception.* Or: *They were all in good time for the conference but late for the reception.*

Beware, when dealing with conjunctions, of putting the comma in the wrong place.

Death was the parson's business, not a subject for social workers but, in an age without God, social workers have stolen the priests' power. The comma after the *but* instead of before it leads us to anticipate that the sense is *but rather*. (However, if we put the comma in the right position we may readily see that it ought to be a semicolon.)

Two-part sentences joined by *and* sometimes dispense with the comma for the sake of effect. *Weekend temperatures soared and beaches were packed* strictly demands a comma, but it would be a pedantic one.

Some writers use commas like seasoning: they seem to feel that a handful of them scattered over the page will bring out the flavour. Others are so nervous of misplacing commas that they avoid them altogether. (A letter from a major insurance company, as transmitted by a broker to his client, explained the complete absence of punctuation in a policy document: 'They have found that the absence of punctuation is a lesser crime than that of wrong punctuation. They have had experience where clerks have inserted the commas in the wrong places which has caused them unexpected expenses.')

The way to avoid over-abundance on the one hand and over-frugality on the other is to make a conscious effort to call upon commas only when they have something to contribute, as for instance:

• To mark off a parenthetical phrase, as discussed, or a parenthetical adverb: *You, perhaps, think otherwise* (a form which puts more weight on *you* than *Perhaps you think otherwise*, which doesn't require a comma). Some adverbs like being enclosed in commas more than others. *However* still often takes commas; so too, but less so, does *therefore*; *too*, however, increasingly dispenses with them.

• To mark off an introductory phrase: *Because of the continuing hot weather, conditions for London commuters can only get worse*. (A comma in this position can often prevent ambiguity creeping in: try re-reading that sentence without one.)

• To divide a compound or complex sentence into manageable proportions (but only after having assimilated the note below on the wrong use of commas). Better, though, to break the indigestible wodge down into manageable sentences.

• To present a list or catalogue: *The chief punctuation marks are comma, semicolon, colon and full stop*. Note that when the last item is prefixed by *and*, the penultimate item does not take a comma, unless to leave it out would cause confusion, as in *Mark, Matthew and John are here*, where the observation might be addressed to Mark; *Mark, Matthew, and John are here* makes it plain that all three are here. *She is the vainest, most selfish, most aggravating woman in the world*. Note that the last item is not followed by a comma.

• To denote a small pause wherever your ear

tells you there is need of one – for example, after *Dear Sir*; to separate descriptive phrases as in *Lord Callaghan, a former Prime Minister, said*; to catalogue a series of happenings, as in *I stopped, looked and listened*; and anywhere else where you would pause naturally were you speaking instead of writing.

Equally as important as knowing where to use a comma is knowing where not to use one. Perhaps the most common abuse is in trying to link two independent sentences that are not already joined by a conjunction: *Uncle Charlie and Auntie Alice arrive today, they will expect to be given lunch.* Here the comma is taking on the duty of a full stop or semi-colon.

Commas must not intrude on clauses that are not supposed to be marked off or parenthesized. *Uncle Charlie and Auntie Alice, who are arriving today, will expect to be given lunch* is fine. *Visitors, who expect to be given lunch, should arrive on time* is not.

Do not let commas stray into any phrase that stands on its own. *Uncle Charlie and Auntie Alice having arrived on time, they were given lunch* makes proper use of a comma. *Uncle Charlie and Auntie Alice, having arrived on time, they were given lunch* brings in an extra comma where it has no right to be and makes a non-sentence.

Above all, never introduce a comma simply to allow a long sentence to get its second wind: *The police were given a strong warning yesterday to adhere to the official guidelines, as it was revealed that serious complaints against the service had risen by 14 per cent*. The comma's only business there is to act as a leaning post, but in pausing for breath the sentence renders its *as* ambiguous. It is supposed to be a concurrent *as* (*just as*); instead, it could easily be taken for a consequential *as* (*because*). The sentence is not over-long and had it kept its nerve could perfectly have done without a comma. True, there are long-winded sentences that seem to cry out for commas, as a marathon runner may gasp for water. Both would be better served by a shorter route to the finishing post.

Semicolon

For some reason – possibly because of the decline of the colon in public esteem – the semicolon is widely regarded as being next to the full stop in the punctuation mark pecking order. In reality it is next to the comma. The comma is a short pause and the semicolon a slightly longer one.

The semicolon can do what a comma can't without the help of a conjunction; as this example shows, it can link two sentences which while independent are nevertheless closely connected.

A semicolon rather than a comma before a conjunction lengthens the pause and strengthens the significance: *The Vicar gave the longest sermon I have ever heard; and not only the longest but the silliest*.

The semicolon comes in very useful in

longish catalogue sentences: *Demanding new curbs on football hooligans, he called for a compulsory registration scheme for soccer fans; a ban on fans travelling to away matches without tickets; and guard dogs for protection of police.* Note that the *and* does not absolve the sentence from its final semicolon, as many are wont to imagine; without the semicolon we have fans being required to have tickets and guard dogs about their persons.

Where the catalogue is introduced by a colon, as in *He demanded these curbs on football hooligans:*, then the semicolons should be regarded as compulsory.

With the merciful decline of over-punctuation, semicolons are used much less than they were; it is possible, nowadays, to read a magazine from cover to cover without coming across a single semicolon. Yet it is easy, once you get the taste for them, to become so addicted that they begin to replace full stops, and you find yourself stringing three or four sentences together as if with paperclips. Use the semicolon sparingly.

Colon

In its main function as the fullest stop before the full stop itself, the colon, despite all evidence to the contrary in these pages, has fallen into disuse. It was most useful for linking two connecting sentences, a task now largely assigned to the semicolon. However, the colon is still often used where the second half of the link explains the first: *This was her weakness: she could never say no*; and where the two halves of a sentence are in antithesis, the standard textbook example being *Man proposes: God disposes*.

Otherwise the colon's main purpose, as Fowler graphically puts it, is 'that of delivering the goods that have been invoiced in the preceding words'. That is, for example, to mark off a prefatory phrase (*To sum up:*); to introduce a list (*The following have arrived:*); to introduce a quotation long enough to warrant a new paragraph (otherwise make do with a comma); to substitute for *for example*, as in *There was every kind of cheese imaginable: Brie, Camembert* etc. But do not insert a colon between a verb and its object: *The principal considerations were: accessibility, proximity to main plant* etc. There should be no punctuation mark of any kind after *were*.

Full stop
The full stop should be the most-used punctuation mark on any page. If your commas regularly out-number your full stops, then your sentences are too long. Be careful, however, of what Fowler calls spot plague – the staccato effect produced by too many short sentences in a row.

Watch for any tendency for two sentences to dispense with their separating full stop by the substitution of a conjunction, comma or semicolon. *He was here only a moment ago; did you know his dog had died?* is two separate thoughts, for all that they concern the same person, and so there must be two separate sentences.

The full stop's secondary role is in abbreviation – or not, as the case may be. Abbreviation full stops have been gradually phasing themselves out over the years: what used to be *M.P.* is now *MP*, *U.K.* is *UK*, *Prof.* has become *Prof* and so on. Although a famous London bookshop meticulously punctuates its postcode as W.C.2.H.O.E.B. it is doubtful whether anyone else does. Use full stops on the initials of proper names – *T.J. Brown Esq* – otherwise avoid cluttering up abbreviations with dots unless the effect of leaving them out is disconcerting, as in *e.g.*

Dash and hyphen

The dash is the versatile understudy for several other punctuation marks – notably (as here) the colon when introducing a list; the semicolon when separating linked sentences where one is consequential to the other, as in *She didn't say yes – but she didn't say no*; and the bracket.

It is not always easy to decide when to choose dashes in preference to brackets. Perhaps parenthetical phrases enclosed in dashes tend to be more tangential than those marked off by brackets. Compare: *The headmaster himself (with whom, by the way, I got on famously) escorted me to the car park* and *The headmaster himself – did you know he was born in Wigan, by the way? – escorted me to the car park*. On the face of it, since they both enclose 'by the way', the two sets of parentheses could be interchanged and no harm done; yet on closer consideration both are appropriate to their particular interjections. The bracketed passage, though an aside, is in context; the passage within dashes is a jaunty irrelevance. But this rather tenuous proposition could be overturned by a dozen other examples. The only rule is to go for what seems most apposite.

Outside their parenthetical purpose, dashes are best used for dramatic effect, as a kind of 'wait for it' pause: *The footman threw open the door, we all rose, and in walked – the cat.*

Dashes should not be used when other stops are capable of doing the job better. *Robert – the man we met in the pub – will be coming* is legitimate. *Robert – who is a friend of Rose – will be coming* would be better served by commas.

Dashes scattered about indiscriminately in the manner of Mr Pickwick's Jingle can be very disconcerting to the reader. *Whether it's bangers and mash for tea – exotic flavours for a barbecue – or the true gourmet touch for a special dinner party – the choice of ingredients is endless.* Not that they would much improve the sense of this breathless advertisement, but all the dashes should be commas.

Coming to the dash as hyphen, the idea of this little device is to enable two or three words to be read as one. This is another area where the tendency is towards redundancy. At one time we would write *to-day, to-morrow* and *sea-side*, and aerodromes became *air-ports* before they were airports. While some word clusters like *mother-in-law*, *do-it-yourself*, *point-to-point*, *Johnny-come-lately* will probably always take hyphens, the usual pattern is for the hyphen to be dropped once we are familiar with a new word combination like *tailback*, *offbeat*, *handbook*. Go by popular usage.

Do not hyphenate unnecessarily. *Chat show*, *badly off*, *colour blind*, not *chat-show*, *badly-off*, *colour-blind*. (Purists insist that leaving the hyphen out of, say, *sitting room* gives us a room that sits. No one in his right mind would believe that a room could sit, but it is as well to be on the alert for ambiguities.)

An adjective or noun qualifying a verb, as in *small-minded*, *hand-operated*, usually takes a hyphen, but an adverb qualifying a verb, as in *highly praised*, does not need to be hyphenated unless omitting the hyphen could distort the meaning. As Sir Ernest Gowers points out, a *fried fish merchant* could be someone other than a *fried-fish merchant*.

Hyphens often set up problems. If you write *second-hand* and *car salesman*, should you write *second-hand-car salesman*, which is fussy, or *second-hand car salesman*, which suggests that the salesman is second-hand? Fruitless hours can be spent pondering such questions. There is no hard and fast solution. It is usually better to leave all the hyphens out than to allow them to pile up.

Brackets

Only three things need to be said about brackets. Do not open parentheses without having the closing bracket in sight. A bracketed passage that is too long for its own good – sometimes longer than the sentence containing it – is likely to lose the reader. A bracketed passage containing more than one sentence is almost certainly too long.

Do not bracket material that demands to stand on its own. *The Duke of Windsor (as King he made the famous remark 'Something must be done' about social conditions in Wales) was not otherwise a political animal* is wrong on two counts. The bracketed passage should be a sentence or clause in its own right; and the sentence itself cannot refer directly to what is sealed off by brackets.

Use brackets sparingly. Like dashes, they can become a bad habit.

Apostrophe

The apostrophe was once regarded as such a utilitarian device that grammar books hardly bothered to mention it. Today, possibly the most common difficulty in written English is with the aberrant apostrophe.

Usually it is shoved in where it has no right to be, as in *it's* (when it should be *its*, meaning belonging to *it*). Often it is omitted where it ought to have been inserted – *ladies* shoes instead of *ladies'* shoes. Sometimes it confuses the plural with the singular – *lady's* shoes, or even *ladie's* shoes. Greengrocers, for some reason, are extremely generous with their apostrophes – *banana's*, *tomatoe's* (or *tom's*), *orange's* etc. Perhaps these come over in crates of fruit, like exotic spiders.

Some would argue that for what it does for the language, the apostrophe is more trouble than it is worth. It may be, in time, that it will wither away – or rather, that the withering-away process will continue. Tennyson, we have to remember, wrote '*Their's* not to reason why', and *Harrods* used to call itself *Harrod's*, while *Earls Court* was *Earl's Court*. The display advertisements in newspapers increasingly dispense with apostrophes alto-gether (except in local papers, where they are still scattered indiscriminately like currants in a bun). But while the apostrophe lasts, the rules governing it are easy enough to master.

The apostrophe's main use is to distinguish the possessive (*prisoner's* friend, *radio's* role) from the plural (*prisoners, radios*). The apostro-phized *'s* was originally a contraction of the old suffix *es*, and it is still used to indicate omitted letters (*wouldn't, let's, B'ham*). It may also be used – sparingly, please – to clarify: *mind your p's and q's*, but, nowadays, *MPs*, not *MP's*, and the *1890's* have given way to the *1990s*.

These incidental apostrophes are simple enough. The possessive apostrophe is only a little less straightforward.

Unlike every other kind of noun, personal pronouns do not take an apostrophe – thus *his, hers, ours, yours, theirs*, and the trouble-some *its* which is often confused with *it's* (meaning *it is*). *Whose*, not *who's*. But other impersonal pronouns are apostrophized (*one's*, *somebody's*, *anybody's*).

Where the possessor is singular (*lady*, *Jones*), the apostrophe always goes before the *s* (*lady's*, *Jones's*). Where she, he or it is plural, the apostrophe goes after the final *s* (*ladies'*, the *Joneses'*) unless the possessors do not possess one (*men*, *women*, *society*), in which case the apostrophe brings the possessive *s* to the word and precedes it (*men's*, *women's*, *society's*).

Those who have been writing *Jones'* for years may look askance at *Jones's*. Singulars ending in *s* – *St James*, *the boss*, *Francis* – did once take their apostrophe without an additional *s* (*St James'*), but now they commonly follow the rule applying to any other singular (*St James's*, *the boss's*, *Francis's*). There remain one or two exceptions, mostly poetical, biblical or pedantic, but for most of us, this obscure area is our Achilles' heel.

Inverted commas
The main use of inverted commas is as quotation marks to wrap around direct speech or a quotation from a text. 'Single' quotes are these days preferred to "double", although the double marks should be used for a quote within a quote, where the person you are quoting throws in a quotation from someone else.

As to where other punctuation marks come in relation to quotation marks, there seems to be no hard and fast rule. Some writers put their stops and commas within the inverted commas, others outside, while others again do a mix. You should be on safe ground if you follow the style of these examples:

• *'Where a piece of dialogue is attributed at its end, conclude it with a comma before you close your inverted commas,' he said.*

• *He added, 'But where the dialogue is attributed at its start, conclude with a full stop inside your inverted commas.'*

• *'The same applies when the dialogue stands on its own.'*

• *But where you are quoting not a whole speech but what may be called 'a fragment of dialogue', put the comma outside the closing quotation mark.* (If this inconsistency bothers you, no harm will come of placing the comma inside the quotes.)

• *'Where a quotation frames a question, does the question mark come within the inverted commas?'* Obviously. The same goes for exclamation marks. But where the question is posed not by the person quoted but by the person quoting, the question mark goes outside the inverted commas: *What does the author mean by 'the question mark goes outside the inverted commas'?*

Some other uses of inverted commas:

• To introduce a new or unusual expression. In the mid Fifties, tabloid headlines would refer to the latest *'Rock'* star. As soon as the reader grows used to the term, the quotation marks are dropped.

• To show that an expression isn't to be taken literally: *The Speaker's 'pigeon loft' in the Palace of Westminster is to be made available to space-cramped MPs.*

• To identify nicknames or some phrase by which a character is known: *Al 'Scarface' Capone, Jim 'Nick Nick' Davidson.* Not necessary when the subject is usually known by his nickname: *Hurricane Higgins.*

Inverted commas meant to indicate facetiousness are in the same class as an exclamation mark after a joke (see below) and should be avoided. Indeed, inverted commas in any class should be avoided wherever possible. They clutter up the page, and an over-indulgence in them has the visual effect of squashed flies. Do not use inverted commas to distance yourself from a slang or colloquial expression. If you want to say *He was out on his ear*, say it, not *He was 'out on his ear'*.

Question mark

A question mark should be used only on a direct question. *Is this a question?* takes a question mark. *He asked if this was a question* does not. A request, if phrased in question form, needs a question mark: *Would you pass the salt, please?* Perversely, *How dare you!*, while in question form, is an exclamation.

A question mark cannot be omitted on the grounds that the question is rhetorical or that the interrogative verb (*can?, shall?, should?* etc.) is a long way from the end of the sentence. *Can it really be, in the last decade of the*

*twentieth century, that man can fly to the Moon
yet is unable to devise a reliable train service to
Sevenoaks?* is a long question and a rhetorical
one, but it still requires its question mark.

Exclamation mark

The obvious place for an exclamation mark is
on an exclamation: *Well I never!* Many impera-
tive phrases – *Go away!*, *Put that down!* take an
exclamation mark, but a command is not
necessarily an exclamation. *Come here* may or
may not require an exclamation mark,
depending upon the intended tone, but *Come
here at once!* certainly calls for one. Insults and
expletives – *You swine!*, *Damn!* – often call for
an exclamation mark, although they are often
more effective without one: *'What an absolute
swine you are, Roger.'*

Outside these categories, exclamation
marks should be avoided. It is no use soup-
ing up a text with exclamation marks to try to
make it sound exciting. Excitement comes out
of the words themselves, not out of signalling
devices. Never put an exclamation mark on a
joke. If it isn't funny without one, it isn't
funny. The same goes for remarks meant to
be ironic. If the irony would escape the
reader without the exclamation mark, give it
its freedom.

Paragraph

It is not universally recognized, particularly
in the newspaper world, where as often as
not it is used simply to break up slabs of type,
that the paragraph is a punctuation device.

Its function is to provide a breathing-space for both writer and reader. Again we go back to spoken punctuation. If you are narrating a long anecdote you will from time to time reach a point where you want to moisten your lips or interject 'Now' or 'So' to indicate that the story is about to move on from the accumulation of detail so far presented.

Just as there are tight sentences which get to the point and then stop, in contrast to loose sentences which ramble on from one conjunction to the next, so there are tight paragraphs and loose paragraphs. A tight paragraph is where a climax of some kind – the punchline, often – comes at the end, and all else leads up to it. Length has nothing to do with it. H.G. Wells begins a tight paragraph with 'In truth the mastery of flying was the work of thousands . . .' and goes on for over two hundred words before concluding it with '. . . And this is the story one makes, putting this thing with that, of Filmer's life and death.' Had he split his paragraph in two at some appropriate point, he would have had a loose, or open-ended paragraph, followed by a tight one.

So there is no natural length to a paragraph. In telling a story aloud, you could well pause often for dramatic effect, sometimes in bursts of only a few words; but then you could reach a point where your narrative compels you to press on in an uninterrupted flow. On second thoughts, there *is* a natural length to a paragraph, and that is what the text demands of its writer.

Confusions

Of the 450 million people who speak English as their mother tongue, there are probably 100 million given regularly to pointing out that *disinterested* does not mean the same as *uninterested* and that *Hopefully, we shall arrive at noon* means not *We hope to arrive at noon* but *We shall arrive at noon in hope*.

A substantial proportion of the other 350 million go cheerfully through life not knowing the difference between *may* and *might* or between *you and I* and *you and me* and, what is more, not caring. The remainder know vaguely when they are getting something wrong but are hazy about the ground rules.

It may seem niggardly to bother about confusions of this kind, but to the reader or listener they often jar, and that means loss of concentration on what is being said. These little pitfalls are fairly easy to avoid by treading carefully as one approaches them. Here are the more common ones:

Compare with/compare to

You *compare to* if you are putting someone or something in the same class as another: *Shall I compare thee to a summer's day?* You *compare with* if you want to make a comparison, either disparaging or complimentary: *Compared with a summer's day, she was like a wet afternoon in February.*

Full/-ful

The only English word ending in *full* is *full*. All others are *-ful*: *cheerful, grateful, bucketful, bucketsful.* Despite the claims of the advertisement hoardings, it should be *Chocful of goodies*, not *Chocfull of goodies*. But note the difference between, say, *carful* and *car full*. *A carful of passengers sang 'God Save the Queen'* says what you mean it to say; but *A car full of passengers sang 'God Save the Queen'* has the car singing the national anthem.

Is/are

Should it be *What is needed is more guns, What is needed are more guns,* or *What are needed are more guns*? The first option – *is, is* – is the answer. Both verbs refer to the subject (*what*, in the sense of *that thing which is needed*) and not to the object (*guns*). By the same token, *What we need is more guns* is correct, since *more guns* is still the sole item of need; but we would say *What we need are more guns and more butter* since *what* now means *those things which are needed*.

Lay/lie

Hens *lay*. One *lays* a table or *lays* down the law or a dozen of vintage port. The past tense is *laid*, as is the past participle. The present participle is *laying*.

People and animals *lie down*, ships *lie at anchor*, one town may *lie* twenty miles from another, and a *choice may lie* with someone or other. The past tense is *lay*, the past participle is *lain* (not much used these days, the tendency being, slackly, towards *laid*), and the present participle is *lying*.

Less/fewer

An advertisement for *The Independent on Sunday* boasted of 'an editorial team of no less than 83 wordsmiths' – to which a reader responded, 'What a large amount! Let's hope none of them have fewer education than your copywriter.'

Quite. *Less* is about quantity (less *sugar*), while *fewer* is about number (fewer *sugar cubes*).

May/might

The confusion here is heightened by the fact that *might* happens to be the past tense of *may*: instead of *I may have been there* you should say *I might have been there*. In other respects, the two words behave as if they were only distantly related. *May* is about conjecture (*He may have been eaten by lions*) or distinct possibility (*It may snow*); while *might* is about retrospective conjecture, often indignant in tone (*I might have been eaten by lions!*) or remote possibility (*It might snow*). *It may snow* suggests that you have been listening to the weather forecast; *It might snow* suggests that you are looking for an excuse for not going out. You could say *There may be a change of government by Christmas* if that seemed likely to happen, but *There might be a change of government by Christmas* carries the implication that pigs might fly.

As for the difference between *may* and *can*, *can I?* means literally *am I able to?* while *may I?* means *am I allowed to?*

None is/are

Contrary to a grammatical old wives' tale, *none* may be either singular or plural.

• Use *none is* when you mean *not one is* (*None of us is perfect*).

• Use *none are* when you mean *no persons are* or *no things are* (*There are none left*).

Number is/are

Fowler recommends treating *number* as singular when it has a definite article (*The number present was small*) and plural when it has an indefinite article (*A small number were present*).

Shall/will

H.W. and F.G. Fowler's *The King's English* devotes twenty-two pages to the difference between *shall* and *will* – and that without touching on the preference in some northern regions for *will* instead of *shall* (*Will I pour you a cup of tea?*).

In practice, at any rate in informal use, the difference is as often as not blurred by contraction – *I'll, you'll, we'll*. Otherwise, most of us have an instinctive if imprecise idea of when to use which. *Shall* is normally used in the first person (*I shall be getting married on Saturday*) except when the speaker wishes to express consent (*I will*) or determination (*I will marry you come what may*). With these exceptions, *will* is usually used in the second or third person (*Will you marry me?, She will marry him*). The marriage service notwithstanding, the use of *shall* in the second or third person (*The man shall answer: I will*), is generally regarded as a little mannered these days.

Should/would
The small print in the rules for *should* and *would* is roughly the same as that for *shall* and *will*, but here again we tend to get it right mainly by instinct. *Should* in its *would* sense is used only in the first person, and only when followed by an *if*-type qualifier (*I should have gone if I'd been invited – but I would have gone, but I wasn't invited*). *Should* in its *ought to* sense is used in all persons (*You should have come to the party, I should have gone to the party*).

Which/that
The simplest definition is that *which* informs, while *that* defines. *This is the house that Jack*

built. *The house, which Jack built in his spare time, is across the street.*

That should be used without a comma. The clause introduced by *which* is usually enclosed within commas or preceded by one.

That being said (or having said which), *which* is often used for *that* simply because it is easier on the ear, and no harm done. *Render unto Caesar the things which are Caesar's* should strictly speaking be *the things that are Caesar's,* but *which* has a better ring to it. But the two must not be used as simple variants of one another, especially in the same sentence. *This is the house which Jack built* is wrong, but *This is the house which Jack built and that Jill designed* is doubly wrong by being half right.

Who/whom

Whom is not simply a genteel way of saying *who.* To put it into grammatical shorthand, *who* is the subject, *whom* the object: the words equate with *he* and *him* – or, for that matter, *I* and *me, she* and *her, we* and *us,* and *they* and *them*: *He* (subject) *will come with me* (object), therefore *Who* (subject) *will come with me? I* (subject) *will go with him* (object), therefore *With whom* (object) *shall I* (subject) *go?* We get the same result with *She will come with us* or *We will go with her (Who will come/go with whom?).*

To simplify the distinction further, think of it only in terms of *he* and *him.* You would say *I didn't know he would be there,* and so it would have to be *I didn't know* who *would be there. I didn't see him there,* and so *Whom did you see there?* Juggle more complex sentences around until you can make the *he/him* comparison. Should it be *There is no one who I would rather see*? No; because you would say *There is no one I would rather see than him* (which shows that you could have done without the *whom* in the first place). Of course, this rule of thumb could break down for anyone unsure between *he* and *him*. Try the test the other way round. Should it be *Who's he?* or *Who's him*? The answer is in *Who's Who*, not *Who's Whom.*

You and I/You and me
This is a common hazard. Even highly educated people often confuse *me* with *I* – sometimes, it has to be said, on purpose: few people these days would answer *It is I* when asked who is at the door.

We are in the same area as *who/whom*, the difficulty being that *you* does not change its form: *I* is subject, *me* object, and so we know where we are, but *you* can be either subject or object. Therefore, in deciding between *you and I* and *you and me*, forget about *you*. If it is *I know the truth*, then it is *You and I know the truth*. If *The truth is known to me*, then *The truth is known to you and me*. The same test holds good with *you and they/you and them, you and he/you and him*, and *you and she/you and her.*

And hopefully . . .

Administer, not *administrate*.

Affect (verb) is to influence. *Effect* (verb) is to bring about. *Effect* (noun) is the outcome.

Aggravate means to make worse, not to irritate.

Alibi is not an excuse but a plea of having been elsewhere at a relevant time. Wrong use: *His alibi was that he was too ill to come.* Right use: *His alibi was that he was in Australia at the time.*

Allegedly does not mean reportedly. *A five-foot squid has allegedly been spotted by divers at Lyme Bay* means either that there is no proof that the squid has been spotted or that the proof has yet to be established.

All right, not *alright*.

Alternate means every other. *Alternative* is a choice. Strictly speaking there can be only two alternatives, but nowadays it is common to hear of several alternatives.

Appraise – form a judgement. *Apprise* – inform.

Beside – next to. *Besides* – as well as.

Comprehensive – exhaustive. *Comprehensible* – intelligible.

Continual – repeated. *Continuous* – uninterrupted.

Definite – free of uncertainty. *Definitive* – authoritative.

Depreciate – fall in value. *Deprecate* – disparage.

Disinterested – impartial. *Uninterested* – not interested.

Enervate does not mean energize, it means its opposite.

Exhaustive – comprehensive. *Exhausted* – tired.

Fortuitous – accidental. *Fortunate* – lucky.

Imply – suggest. *Infer* – deduce.

Licence is a noun, *license* a verb.

Like has several definitions, none of which is *such as*. *There was a display of fruit like oranges, pineapples and grapefruit* is saying there was a display of fruit similar in character or appearance to oranges etc.

Luxuriant – abundant. *Luxurious* – opulent.

Mayhem does not mean murder, but great disorder.

Practical – opposite of theoretical. *Practicable* – capable of being carried out. *A practical man. A practicable plan.*

Practice is a noun, *practise* a verb.

Predication must not be confused with *prediction*: it means a logical statement.

Principal (noun) – head; (adjective) – most important. *Principle* – doctrine.

Stationary – not moving. *Stationery* – paper and envelopes.

Verbal does not mean the same as oral. *Oral* – expressed with the mouth. *Verbal* – expressed in words. Thus *verbal sex* would mean talking about it.

Relaxations

Browse through any piece of writing from two hundred, one hundred, even twenty or thirty years ago: never mind whether it is from a work of literature or an advertisement for soap, you will see how radically the language has changed, along with practically everything else.

Like our dress and manners generally, written English has gradually become more and more informal, following the tendency of spoken English towards the universally colloquial verging on the slangy. While this continuing process of relaxation accommodates a good deal of regrettable slapdashery, the language is on balance the healthier for adapting to the times it lives in. For the written word to resist change would be for literature to fossilize itself, and we should end up with a form of High English bearing little resemblance to the way people speak, and therefore having little contact with the way they live.

As an example of how the world turns grammatically speaking, Fowler fulminates for two pages in *Modern English Usage* (1926) against what he termed the *fused participle*, the ungrammatical use of a noun with a participial phrase as in – to coin an example – *Writers knowing about grammar improves their style*. Technically this should be, if it is going to be anything, *Writers'* (possessive) *knowing about grammar improves their style*, in that what we are saying is that knowing about grammar by writers improves their style. There is little point in going into Fowler's demolition of this construction, since so many of the instances he quotes are now everywhere paralleled – and preferred: *We need fear nothing from China* (should be China's) *developing her resources*; *It is no longer thought to be the proper scientific attitude to deny the possibility of anything* (should be anything's) *happening*. Fowler comments: 'A dozen years ago, it was reasonable, and possible without much fear of offending reputable writers, to describe as an 'ignorant vulgarism' the more elementary form of the fused participle, i.e. that in which the noun part is a single word, and that a pronoun or proper name; it was not very easy to collect instances of it.'

With trembling respect to the master of English usage, this perfectly phrased denunciation must in part trouble some present-day readers almost as much as the offending fused participle did Fowler and some of his contemporaries. That sub-clause *and that a pronoun or proper name,* meaning *that single word being a pronoun* etc., is a sophisticated form of construction which most of us no longer use. It is our loss. Yet we may presumptuously suppose that Fowler, who had to be read twice only when he was guiding his readers through some of the more arcane swamps of English syntax, would for a modern audience have tailored that passage to the less complex usage of the day – although he may have grumbled on to the last about his fused participles.

One reason we no longer fuss over fused participles is that there is so much more to make a fuss about – for example, the wording of a plaque which graces many an executive desk in Britain and America: *Press on. Nothing in the world can take the place of perseverance. Talent will not; Nothing is more common than unsuccessful men with talent. Genius will not; Unrewarded genius is almost a proverb. Education alone will not; The World is full of educated derelicts. Perseverance and determination alone are omnipotent.* To brood on the readiness of men at the top of their professions to lap up such syntactical and stylistic balderdash is to despair of the English language – as it is, to take another example, to stand on a railway platform and contemplate this British Rail poster: *My son didn't tell me – I found out about his fare fiddling through a court letter – I shouldn't have opened it I know – but why didn't he tell me. Then I found out why in court – he'd been doing it for ages – he's got to pay it all back plus the fine –*

he can't of course. And a criminal record. No job and this won't help. So what now? I don't know, things have changed haven't they.

They have indeed. Fortunately there is a happy medium, and it is in that body of relaxed yet tolerably literate English that is by now the norm. We no longer worry about whether it is permissible to say *none are* and *different to* (not that we need have worried in the first place, since authorities allow us both supposed deviations – although they will still not give us *different than*). We do not unduly concern ourselves with split infinitives or, given that a GCSE English paper instructs candidates to 'think carefully who you are writing for', with *who/whom* or ending a sentence with a preposition. We have lost the distinction between *each other* and *one another*. We use *only* in the wrong place, as in *He only arrived yesterday*, which really means *He alone arrived yesterday*. We speak (following the example of Dickens) of *our mutual friend* when we mean *our common friend*. We switch from *one* to *you* in the same sentence. We say *the reason is because* when we should say *the reason is that* (*because* itself means *for the reason that*). *He was sat* for *he was sitting* and *try and* for *try to* now pass unnoticed. We allow *due to* to stand in for *owing to* (*due*, being an adjective, should by rights be attached to a noun). We confuse *populace* (common people) with *population*, and *however, whatever, whoever* with *how ever?, what ever?, who ever?* Most of us were not even aware that *reliable, actionable* and some other *-able* forms were once an affront to the language, on the grounds (Fowler again) that to speak of a *reliable man* or an *actionable offence* is to say that we *rely a man* or *act an offence*.

Some of these lapses are more reprehensible than others, and to be avoided; yet they no longer represent the unacceptable face of English grammar. Among reasonably literate people, the consensus (not *general consensus*, as tautology would have it) seems to be that anything is permissible that does not offend the senses. We have yet to reach the day when *children who you or your spouse get child benefit for* on a supposedly 'plain English' retirement pension form is tolerable to all who read it; and *Your spouse if they are not getting their own retirement pension* on the same form could have been better put as *Your spouse, if not getting a retirement pension*.

And so English no longer necessarily has to be on its best grammatical behaviour to be socially acceptable. We have discussed ellipsis, where all manner of words may be legitimately omitted because they are implied. In these casual times, words are often dropped which grammar still insists must be taken on board. Take words accompanying *than*. Both these examples make sense: *It was more like a video arcade than a library; I'd rather go with Uncle Fred than Uncle Charlie* – but textbooks still prefer *It was more like a video arcade than like a library; I'd rather go with Uncle Fred than with Uncle Charlie*. Unless the omission clouds the sense, for example *I think I know Uncle Fred better than* (I know) *Uncle Charlie*, where it could be Uncle Charlie who claims the better acquaintanceship, harmless excisions of this sort are surely now allowable.

A sentence which misses out its *auxiliary verbs* (verbs such as *have, be, shall* etc. whose main job is to express the voice, tense and mood of other verbs) is supposed to be committing an offence. So it is if the sentence is *I been down the pub*; but you could have a sentence on the lines of *The three main influences which* (may have) *contributed to the success of the club were probably wine, women and song in that order*, and the sin would be not so much its missing auxiliaries (omitted because they are tautological with *probably*) as its clumsy construction. Better by far to recast such a sentence than to insist on its taking its grammatical medicine: *Probably the three main influences contributing to the success of the club* etc. When it comes to missing out auxiliary verbs, the test should be (a) does it make sense? and (b) does it read well? *The question was whether he* (should) *go or stay* fulfils both qualifications. *The problem was whether he* (should have) *stayed or departed: now he wished he had gone* fulfils neither (but had its *was* been *had been*, it could have done without its *should have*).

We have looked at confused and fused participles. Grammar, in the shape of Eric Partridge's *Usage and Abusage*, declares that

Completely surrounded by a deep wide moat, access to it was only possible by a brick bridge is wrong, as we already know. Yet if the alternative is *The house being completely surrounded by a deep wide moat* etc., when obviously the house must already have been identified in the previous sentence, then perhaps today's abusage (actually, the example dates back to 1924) may on occasion be preferable to yesterday's usage. If the sentence is short and incapable of misinterpretation, for example *Growing up in the war years, his education was ramshackle*, then it could be excusable.

Far more troublesome than the unnecessary words left out of sentences are the unnecessary words put into them. Phrases on the lines of *by virtue of the fact that* (meaning because), *the question as to whether* (whether), *in the event of* (if), are very often used in the belief that they are the straw with which grammatical bricks are made. Usually they are the means by which grammatical bricks are dropped, in that verbosity of this order goes hand in hand with verbal ineptitude. Long words do not a better sentence make, nor longwindedness perfect syntax. Indeed, the shorter the words and the more straightforward the construction, the likelier is a sentence to be on grammatically firm ground. *While it has not yet proved possible to ascertain whether or not our instructions as received by you were in accordance with the procedure as laid down* . . . is an opening clause on its way to an accident. *We cannot yet say whether the instructions you received followed the standard procedure; however*. . . is a sentence which knows where it is going.

What is so depressing about the *By virtue of the fact that* school is that its output is manifestly the product of sweated labour. While, as some of the best writers would testify, it can be fiendishly hard to write clearly, it should never be a struggle to write grammatically. If a sentence does not seem grammatically sound, it is far better to strip it down and start again than to fiddle about with it in an effort to get the syntax right.

Clearly the following passage (written incidentally by one successful novelist about another) is a syntactical disaster area: *Many years ago he rang up and asked to come and talk about writing a novel as he wanted to go over the outline in greater detail, later sending me proofs before discussing its promotion and indeed it turned out to be a great success.* Just as clearly, any time spent on it would be better devoted to establishing what it is trying to say and then re-working it so that it says it as lucidly as possible, rather than plodding through its grammar. A purely grammatical overhaul would get us something like this: *Many years ago he rang up to ask if he could come and talk about writing a novel, as he wanted to go over the outline in greater detail. Later he was to send me proofs before discussing its promotion with me; and indeed it turned out to be a great success* – which is not much less confusing than the original. Looking at it for sense and clarity yields us *Many years ago he rang me to ask if he could come and talk about the novel he was writing, as he wanted to go over the outline in greater detail. Eventually he sent me proofs, when we discussed its promotion. The novel turned out a great success.* Moral: concentrate on sense and clarity and the sloppy grammar will as likely as not correct itself.

Equally, there is no point in wrestling with grammar when you are unsure what problem you are trying to overcome. Re-cast instead. *I do not like these kind of sweets* seems a simple enough sentence but it has something wrong with it: *these kind* cannot be right. But what should it be? *I do not like these kinds of sweets* seems more like it, but then *kinds* cannot be right either since obviously it is one kind or class of sweets we are talking about. Then what about *I do not like this kind of sweet*? But it happens that we are talking about humbugs and aniseed balls, which are two kinds of sweets. Try *I do not like this kind of sweets*. That happens to be correct, since the adjective has to agree in number with the noun it is pointing out (*kind*); but the non-grammarian may still take some convincing. If he had refused to be bullied by grammar and gone for plain English he would have produced *I do not like sweets of this kind* and said what he wanted to say with no grammatical hassle whatsoever.

Clarity and sound, not grammar, should finally govern the construction of a sentence. That is why we drop *that* when grammar, or anyway the grammatical pedant, decrees that it should be present: *She is all I have left* sounds better than *She is all that I have left*. It is why we say *No one is as bad a sailor as me* instead of *No one is as bad a sailor as I*. If the sense is there, let the sound be the judge of how it expresses itself. Heed the words of Raymond Chandler to one of his editors: 'Would you convey my compliments to the purist who reads your proofs and tell him or her that I write in a sort of broken-down patois which is something like the way a Swiss waiter talks, and that when I split an infinitive, God damn it, I split it so it will stay split.' Or as Philip Howard put it: 'We do not run the English language as a drill-yard for grammarians.'

Part Two

. . . and the Music

The Tin Ear

We know some of the notes: now for the tune.

Of the five senses, the most precious to the writer is the sense of hearing. There have been great blind writers from Homer to Milton and beyond, but no great deaf ones – deaf, that is, as it may be taken to mean being unable to hear one's composition in one's head, as Beethoven heard his music.

The mind dictates what is to be written. The ear monitors what is going down on paper – or at least it should. So many writers and speakers know what they have to say but pay no attention at all to the way they are saying it. They require their audience to listen, yet they do not listen to themselves.

When a Chancellor of the Exchequer can say *We're not in the business and I'm not going to be tempted to forecast interest rates precisely*, he knows what he means but he does not realize that he has started one sentence (*We're not in the business*), abandoned it, and then opted for another, because he is not listening to his own voice. The estate agent who advertises a *delightful flat – ideal for being so close to Kensington High Street* may be surprised to hear that he is on grammatically firm ground, in that *ideal for* demands either a noun or a participle, and *being so close to Kensington High Street* is a participial phrase; but it is a clumsy one, which no one would perpetrate who had any ear for English.

Encountering a passage of written English by someone who does not have an ear for the language is like hearing a soprano singing flat. You do not have to be technically informed to know that it sounds all wrong.

Everyday examples abound. Here is part of an advertisement for an 'elegant mahogany-finish mobile library': *You may move it around without difficulty thanks to hidden castors. The top will, of course, take a lamp, photographs, plant and miscellany that's important to you.*

Its eccentric punctuation notwithstanding, there is nothing grammatically wrong with this piece of copywriting – it is just that its author has a tin ear. While it may be taking a sledgehammer to a nut, it should prove useful to pull it to pieces and analyse exactly what is wrong with it.

With a comma after *difficulty*, the first sentence would just about pass muster, although it could usefully be shortened to *It is easy to move around, thanks to hidden castors*; or, the better to avoid the dying fall of this construction, *Thanks to hidden castors, it is easy to move around*.

The second sentence is a mess. The copy-writer's disconcerting trick of dodging from the singular to the plural and back again – *a lamp, photographs, plant* – is as unsettling for the audience as a pianist changing key twice within three bars. Giving *a lamp* but not *plant* an indefinite article does nothing for the rhythm of the sentence, while the abstract *miscellany* sits uneasily with its concrete companions, the *lamp, plant* and *photographs*. Miscellany of what, anyway? The commas marking off *of course* are superfluous, as indeed, come to think of it, is the expression *of course* itself.

As for *that's important to you*, the phrase is so lame and inept that it reads like a bad translation from the Serbo-Croat. It is evidently there because the writer ran out of things to say before reaching the end of his sentence, but had to bring it to a stop somehow. It does not aim for effect, it does not inform, it makes no effort to grab the reader's interest, it simply tails off like someone aimlessly humming a tune he does not know all the way through. Nor can it withstand a second's scrutiny. The top of the 'mobile library' will take *a miscellany that's important to you*. A miscellany is a mixture of various things. A mixture of various important things could mean your insurance policies, your wedding ring, your cheque book and the dog.

Enough of this. Let us relieve this bungling piece of advertising copy of its embarrassment by rephrasing it in English that has been listened to as it was set down on paper: *Thanks to hidden castors, it is easy to move around. The top will take a lamp, a plant, photographs, or anything you want to display.*

The revision may not sell 'mobile libraries' but at least it does not offend the ear.

But a piece of writing does not necessarily have to be downright ugly to fail the aural test. A passage may scan perfectly well and yet come over as leaden. If it is a dull sentence it will be a drag on the narrative, while if it is an out-and-out lifeless one – grammatically sound, but constructionally brain-dead – it will defy the reader's most earnest efforts to understand what it is driving at.

This sentence from a newspaper report seems straightforward enough, yet it cannot be read without a sense of vague confusion: *The cuts would mean the loss of all nursery and adult education, school catering and 600 teachers' jobs, the closure of all children's day centres, and a quarter of all homes for children, the elderly and mentally handicapped.*

Had the writer sounded out these words for sense and style as well as for factual content, he could have turned up the several flaws that prevent their message getting across. It is worth examining in detail how this sentence loses its reader.

In the first place the abrupt switch from general quantity (*nursery and adult education, school catering*) to specific number (*600 teachers' jobs*) is unsettling and should be smoothed out. Then there is a muddle over the transition from the first half of the sentence, which is governed by the word *loss*, to the latter half which is governed by *closure*. This can only be cleared up by the insertion of a conjunction between the two halves; it was presumably left out because the writer felt he was overdoing his *and*s. Finally, because of this sentence's cavalier way with commas, bestowing or withholding them at will, there is a little ambiguity over whether *the elderly and mentally handicapped* are one and the same or two separate categories. To be far-fetched, the way the sentence is cast it could even be talking about *the loss of the elderly and mentally handicapped*.

These are the repair requirements to make the passage understandable at first reading:

• The reiteration of an *all* before *school catering*, plus a comma after it, to mark up the distinction between the quantitative *nursery and adult education and school catering* and the numerical *teachers' jobs*;

• The insertion of a conjunction to mark the change from *loss* to *closure*. If the writer feels this would be one *and* too many, then let him have a *plus* instead, which would strengthen the differentiation between the two classes;

• The omission of the comma after *children's day centres*. The presence of the comma makes the sentence read as if the last item on its list is defined by the *and* before *mentally handicapped*. It isn't. The last item on the list is *a quarter of all homes* etc., *a quarter of all* being the final category after all;

• The insertion of *the* before *mentally handicapped* to make it clear that *the elderly and mentally handicapped* are not one entity.

The sentence now reads: *The cuts would mean the loss of all nursery and adult education, all school catering, and 600 teachers' jobs, plus the closure of all children's day centres and a quarter of all homes for children, the elderly and the mentally handicapped.*

(If we are to look at the content of the sentence as well as its style, it could be improved still further by putting *600 teachers' jobs* at the head of the list before *nursery and adult education and school catering*, on the grounds that the concrete is always more arresting than the abstract.)

Over and above the grammatical restrictions put upon it, and besides its obligations to avoid the Seven Deadly Sins of composition described in another section, there are still several classic ways in which a piece of writing can find itself in trouble, provided its creator has not, so to speak, played it back to himself, listened to its cadences, and identified the flat notes. These are *false emphasis* (stressing the wrong clause); *anti-climax* (putting the least interesting fact last); *wrong direction* (misleading the reader as to the writer's intention); *wrong rhythm* (giving the reader an unintended jolt); *wrong order* (too much distance between companion words); *over-*

punctuation (usually too many commas); and *dead wood* (too many auxiliaries and other superfluous words).

Let us now take a sentence at random from *War and Peace*, and then see how it might have been mauled in the wrong hands:

> *Next day old Kutusov, having been called very early, said his prayers and dressed, and then got into his chariot with the disagreeable feeling that he had now to direct a battle to be fought against his will.*

This short passage could scarcely be improved upon, even by Tolstoy himself had he been originally writing in English. It is informative, it carries the narrative forward and compels the reader to move on with it, it is lucid, it is elegant in style, and it is graphic in the images it conjures up. Furthermore it does not waste a word – but there are worse transgressions a sentence might commit than word-wasting.

False emphasis

> *Having been called very early the next day, old Kutusov said his prayers and dressed, and then got into his chariot with the disagreeable feeling that he had now to direct a battle to be fought against his will.*

Tolstoy's sentence is now setting off on the wrong foot. It gives undue emphasis to *having been called very early* by promoting it from a subordinate clause between parenthetical commas to the opening participial clause which is supposed to colour the whole sentence. The fact of Kutusov's having been called early is comparatively incidental; here it becomes paramount.

Anti-climax
> *With the disagreeable feeling that he had now to direct a battle to be fought against his will, Kutusov, having been called very early and said his prayers and dressed, then got into his chariot.*

This construction follows the mistaken notion that the most important information must always come first. In newspaper journalism, perhaps it should. In other forms of writing, it is often more effective for the most important fact to be presented last: *I came, I saw, I conquered.* The effect here is that having presented its juiciest morsel up front, the sentence has little of comparable interest to offer, and so it finishes lamely, leaving the reader with a feeling of let-down.

Wrong direction
> *Next day, having been called very early, old Kutusov said his prayers and dressed, and then got into his chariot with the disagreeable feeling that he had now to direct a battle to be fought against his will.*

This is a mix of *false emphasis* and *anti-climax*. The first half of the sentence travels at far too leisurely a pace for the second half, giving the reader the impression that it is to be a reflective sort of sentence with not a great deal happening in it. With this construction, Kutusov's getting into his chariot and going off to battle comes as something of a shock – we had been lulled into anticipating that he was about to sit down to breakfast.

Wrong rhythm

Next day old Kutusov, having been called very early and said his prayers and dressed, then got into his chariot with the disagreeable feeling that he had now to direct a battle to be fought against his will.

All we have done is to lose a comma and shift the *and* from in front of *then got into his chariot* to before *said his prayers*, but it is enough to tilt the sentence off balance. Where it led the reader smoothly along, it now stumbles. Even the untouched second half of the sentence now no longer feels comfortable – suddenly it seems to go on a beat too long, while the repetition of *to* in *to direct a battle to be fought* suffers from the aftereffects of that earlier misplaced *and*. Whether misapplied or wrongly withheld, ill-judged conjunctions and commas will always affect the weight of one sentence component against another. Rhythm is mainly about putting words and punctuation marks in the right places so that they don't jut out like loose paving stones to trip up the reader as he travels from one end of a sentence to the other.

Wrong order

> *Next day old Kutusov, having been called away early, said his prayers and dressed, and then, with the disagreeable feeling that he had now to direct a battle to be fought against his will, got into his chariot.*

Old Kutusov is far too far away from his chariot. This kind of construction, which stretches the distance between two closely related things almost to breaking-point, is very common among inexperienced writers, who probably feel they are giving value for money by stuffing the sentence with as much detail as it will hold, and more, before marrying subject and object. Closely related words should remain close: not *The Minister, to assess the effects of the controversial new guidelines at factory floor level, has called in industrial advisers* but *The Minister has called in industrial advisers to help him assess* etc.

Over-punctuation

> *Next day, old Kutusov, having been called very early, said his prayers and dressed, and then, got into his chariot, with the disagreeable feeling that he had now to fight a battle, to be fought against his will.*

Tolstoy has three commas serve thirty-eight words. Sprinkle those words with unnecessary commas and the flow is hampered, the sense impaired. Over-punctuation is a sign of the writer's under-confidence in his grasp of syntax: he uses commas like crutches to help his sentences limp along.

Dead wood

> *The next day old Kutusov, having been called very early, and having said his prayers and then got dressed, then got into his chariot with the disagreeable feeling that he had now got to direct a battle which was to be fought against his will.*

Over-punctiliousness with the grammatical niceties is a similar affliction (or addiction) to over-punctuation and displays the same lack of confidence, assuming as it does that the reader will not be able to find his way to the end of the sentence without a signpost at every corner. In the supposed interests of clarity, Tolstoy's thirty-eight words have here stretched to forty-five.

Let us now, to drive the lesson home, conduct the exercise the other way round and take another sentence from *War and Peace* which has been doctored to accommodate most of the faults listed above. We will then proceed to unravel it. We start with the most extremely garbled version:

> *As between the two sides, in the question of history, the whole difference of view, as was once so in the question of astronomy, is based upon the recognition, or the non-recognition, of some absolute unity; which unity serves as a standard for visible phenomena.*

Dead wood

Removing, to begin with, the five superfluous words we have inserted like cloves
into a baked ham, we are left with:

> *Between the two sides, in the question of*
> *history, the whole difference of view, as once in*
> *the question of astronomy, is based upon the*
> *recognition, or non-recognition, of some*
> *absolute unity; which serves as a standard for*
> *visible phenomena.*

Over-punctuation

We now, changing our metaphor, extract the
grapeshot of stops which has been sprayed
over the sentence, restoring the punctuation
to Tolstoy's original two commas:

> *Between the two sides in the question of history*
> *the whole difference of view, as once in the ques-*
> *tion of astronomy, is based upon the recognition*
> *or non-recognition of some absolute unity*
> *which serves as a standard for visible*
> *phenomena.*

Wrong order

As we chip away the superfluities the second
half of the sentence, like a sculpture taking
shape out of a block of marble, has by now
emerged as Tolstoy wrote it; but there is still a
lot wrong with the first half. For one thing,
the *two sides*, their *difference of view*, and what
that difference *is based upon* are too widely
separated for them to cohere as one idea. Try
this:

> *The whole difference of view between the two sides in the question of history, as once in the question of astronomy, is based upon the recognition or non-recognition of some absolute unity which serves as a standard for visible phenomena.*

Wrong emphasis

It is better, but it will still not do. *The whole difference of view* etc. falling at the beginning of the sentence is top-heavy; it distracts from what it is leading up to. One more adjustment:

> *As once in the question of astronomy, the whole difference of view between the two sides in the question of history is based upon the recognition or non-recognition of some absolute unity which serves as a standard for visible phenomena.*

Wrong rhythm

We are nearly there, but the reduction of Tolstoy's two essential commas to one should tell us, even if the ear does not, that the rhythm of the sentence is not quite right. Its second half sings; its first half still sounds off-key. Let us then go back to how Tolstoy, or his translator, wrote it:

> *As once in the question of astronomy, so now in the question of history, the whole difference of view between the two sides is based upon the recognition or non-recognition of some absolute*

unity which serves as a standard for visible phenomena.

And at last we see how effortlessly effective a piece of writing can be – when a little effort has been put into it.

We do not of course have any idea how many alterations and crossings out went into that sentence before Tolstoy passed on to the next. Probably none: you do not embark upon *War and Peace* without first having developed a certain facility of style. But the whole art of writing depends upon the ability to make it look as if it flowed smoothly from the pen whether it did or not. Some writers compose more easily than others; but there must be very few of them indeed who do not from time to time have to struggle for the right word, or to tinker with the odd sentence, fine-tuning it until, like a musical composition painstakingly being brought to life on the piano keyboard, it finally begins to sing. Sometimes, in exhibitions of authors' notebooks and so on, we are given a glimpse of this re-working process. There is a fascinating facsimile, published a few years ago, of the manuscript of George Orwell's *Nineteen Eighty-four*, complete with all his crossings-out and re-wording. The first sentence, as originally written, reads:

> *It was a cold, blowy day in early April, and innumerable clocks* [this is a substitution for *a million radios*] *were striking thirteen.*

Three deleted words and one additional word later, it becomes:

It was a bright, cold day in April, and the clocks were striking thirteen.

It remained now only for Orwell to delete the comma after *bright* either in the final typescript or in proof, and he had a clean, uncluttered sentence which was to become one of the most memorable opening lines in modern English literature – a distinction it could not have aspired to had he not realized what a dud note was struck by that obtrusive, clumsy *innumerable*, and re-tuned accordingly.

To take finally a less exalted example, where we have the advantage of being privy to the author's thought processes as he made his adjustments, let us consider the opening lines of this section as they appeared in first draft:

We now know some of the notes: now for the tune.

Of all the five senses, the most valuable to the writer is his sense of hearing. There have been many great blind writers, from Homer to Milton and beyond, but no great deaf ones – deaf, that is to say, in the sense of one's being unable to hear one's composition in one's head, as Beethoven listened to his music.

Now for the alterations and the reasoning behind them:

Opening sentence: Omission of *now* in first

clause to avoid repetition (*we now know . . . now for the tune*).

Second sentence: substitution of *precious* for *valuable* as being the more appropriate word. Substitution of *the* for *his*: if *the writer* is to be neuter, the writer's senses should be neuter too.

Third sentence: omission of superfluous comma after *blind writers*. Substitution, in the first instance, of *meaning* for *sense* which is too close to *senses* and *sense* in the previous sentence, where the word means something else. *Meaning*, however, does not settle in at all happily – one cannot really get away with *in the meaning of* – and so the replacement for *in the sense of* becomes *as it may be taken to mean*. Contraction of *that is to say* to *that is*. Omission of the superfluous *one's* in *one's being unable*. Substitution of *as Beethoven heard his music* for *as Beethoven listened to his music*: Beethoven's *heard* is now in harmony with the *hear* of *hear one's composition in one's head*, and the sentence flows the better for it.

Thus tuned, the passage finally reads, at the end of this section, as it does at the beginning:

> *We know some of the notes: now for the tune.*
>
> *Of the five senses, the most precious to the writer is the sense of hearing. There have been great blind writers from Homer to Milton and beyond, but no great deaf ones – deaf, that is, as it may be taken to mean being unable to hear one's composition in one's head, as Beethoven heard his music . . .*

Getting Organized

No one would set about building a garden wall by simply tipping out a barrowload of bricks and setting about cementing them together. But that is how many would-be writers set about putting words together. They plunge in without any preparation and then are put out when the wall falls down.

Writing – every kind of writing from an office memo to a novel – has to be planned and organized. You do hear of writers who are supposed to sit down at the typewriter or word processor without a thought in their heads, tap out the words 'Chapter One' and plunge into their next best seller. Do not believe it. They prepare their work as much as any other writer – it is just that they get into the preparatory process by jumping in at the deep end. Once having got started they will be jotting down notes, drawing up a rough synopsis of at least the first few chapters, and probably scrapping what they have written and starting again.

Writing is a discipline and it should be approached as one. It is difficult to do scrappily, a sentence here and a sentence there, without jerkiness and lack of continuity. Therefore write when you have a good block of time available – preferably not less than a couple of hours.

How you write, whether with pen, pencil, typewriter or word processor, is up to you. There is, however, this to be said against the word processor for first draft original composition if you are not the most fluent of writers: every other means of writing keeps all your options open in that your crossings-out and corrections are all the time visible, so that should you begin to wonder whether an alteration was after all wise, all the alternative versions are there in manuscript in front of you.

Where you write is for circumstance and temperament to decide. Not every writer locks himself in a cork-lined room. There have been novels scribbled at kitchen tables, detective stories written on trains, company reports dictated in the backs of limousines, poems composed in waterlogged trenches, speeches prepared in bathrooms. Much good writing has been produced out of chaos. Chaos, however, does not of itself produce good writing. Neither, it has to be said, do preparation and organization alone. But before you begin to set down your thoughts, it is as well to have them marshalled and ready.

What do you want to say?

A constant characteristic of bad writing is that it has nothing to say. Why some writers feel compelled to write when they have nothing to write about is a mystery. It is like a cook baking a pie with no ingredients. All the effort and all the artistry go into trying to disguise the fact that the pie is empty. But you cannot produce a dish full of steam and call it cookery.

Much of what might be called the arm-twisting school of writing comes into this category. It is where someone has been reluctantly persuaded, or in a rash moment has agreed, to write something – perhaps an article for his club newsletter or a report for the local paper. He puts off the chore until the last possible moment and then finds he has no idea what he wants to say. But the deadline looms. He sets to, and with the maximum of effort produces an empty pie.

Other would-be writers have the urge to write but can think of nothing to write about. The obvious solution is either to go out and find something to write about, or to sit down and recall some event or experience worth reliving on paper. Books on creative writing – of which this manual does not set itself up to be one – always say that the apprentice writer should write of what he knows. This is sound advice, but no formula for getting published. If you are going to write about, for instance, your childhood memories, do it more for your own enjoyment and the enjoyment of your friends than with any great hope of getting into print.

By far the largest class of writers with nothing to say is that substantial body of pen-chewers which did have something to say but never got round to thinking it out. Like the furrowed-browed members of the arm-twisting school, these unfortunates usually come late to their task, when they grapple with their half-formed thoughts in the hope of pinning them down on paper much as an all-in wrestler pins his opponent to the canvas. What they never seem to grasp is that in even the simplest sentence, the thought and the expression of that thought are two separate if closely connected processes. If you cannot write *The boy licked the jam off the spoon* without first being clear in your mind that that is what the boy did, then most certainly you cannot write *Setting the Stonehenge lintels in place was a very labour-intensive task, achieved by the use of levers and stacks of squared-off timbers* without first knowing confidently what you have to say and then finding the best way of expressing it.

The well-prepared writer does not arrive at his desk with the day's quota of words already formed in his mind. What he should have in his mind is an orderly quota of ideas ready for conversion into words.

Make a plan
The only place for a rambling discourse is in a personal letter where a chatty, discursive

style, reflecting the personality of the writer, can work to charming effect. All other forms of writing should follow a plan.

You have, it is to be assumed, by now marshalled your thoughts and know what you want to say. The next step is to jot down your main points, then number them in a logical order – preferably chronologically, unless some other arrangement suggests itself.

If what you have to write depends upon factual information, see that you have all the facts to hand before you start.

You should now have a working synopsis. Expand on it as you write by all means, but do not feel obliged to over-expand simply for the sake of putting flesh on your skeleton. Keep what you have to say concise.

Should you find yourself, when you come to write, departing from your notes, stop and ask yourself why. Are you dealing with matters arising or are you going off up a blind alley? If, in the light of what you have written so far, your notes need revising, then revise them; but unless you are a very experienced traveller do not attempt a journey without maps.

Find the right voice

We all have different styles of writing to suit different occasions. Charged with riding a bicycle without lights, you would not write your excuses to the magistrates' court in the same tone you would adopt in a letter describing the incident to Uncle Charlie. Most people develop three voices – the formal, for official or semi-official communications; the familiar, for correspondence with family and friends; and somewhere in between for any other business, such as letters to the paper, office memos and reports, informal business letters, articles for the house magazine and so on. There is no reason, however, why the three voices should differ in quality just because they differ in tone. Consider the following three extracts:

> Young men, starting out in life, have often asked me, 'How can I become an Internee?' Well, there are several methods. My own was to buy a villa in Le Touquet on the coast of France and stay there till the Germans came along. This is probably the best and simplest system. You buy the villa and the Germans do the rest.

> On July 27th, a Sunday, I went down to the Kommandantur to report. We were informed that we were all to be interned. We were allowed to go home and pack. I went to my home accompanied by a soldier and packed a small hand bag and was taken back to Paris-Plage. My wife was greatly distressed.

> As for finding internment terrible, I didn't at all after the first few months. Loos Prison, Liège Barracks and the Citadel of Huy were on the tough side, but Tost was fine. One thing that helped us enormously there was the presence of the internees from Holland.

They are all from the pen of P.G. Wodehouse. The first is from one of his controversial broadcasts to the United States from Berlin after his release from wartime internment; the second is from a statement to the British authorities explaining the broadcasts; and the third is from a letter to his old friend W. Townend describing his experiences. Here there are three distinct voices: the humorous, familiar to all Wodehouse readers; the serious, consciously devoid of any leavening of humour; and the chattily informal. Yet in a sense they are all the same voice: one that speaks clearly, stylishly and effectively to produce a lively, well-constructed narrative, whatever the context.

Develop your written voice to convey your personality without intruding upon your own text. Except in personal letters, do not be over-familiar – keep a polite distance between you and your reader, even where you are being informal. Be informal without being slangy. Be formal without being pompous: *Subsequent to my four years' experience with British Gaskets I obtained employment in a senior capacity with British Grummets* sounds like evidence in court. *After four years with British Gaskets I joined the senior staff of British Grummets* says what the job applicant wishes to say in a clear, distinctive voice.

The writing stage

Work avoidance is endemic among writers. Even the busiest of professional journalists will find 'essential' tasks such as pencil sharpening and changing light bulbs which must be completed before he can settle down to the day's work.

Such reluctance is understandable. No matter how well-briefed you may be for what you have to write, the moment is about to arrive when you have to buckle down and write it – that is, when you have to summon a succession of words, in more or less the right order, not from some cornucopian source of inspiration but from the ceiling. Yet it has to be faced, and allowing for a modicum of procrastination, it has to be faced head on. The writer who puts off until tomorrow what he should get down to today on the grounds that he is not in the mood or that the words will not come will find himself in an even worse state of creative inertia a week or a fortnight hence.

Along with their work avoidance techniques, all writers have their idiosyncrasies. They can write only with a soft pencil on ruled yellow pads, or they have to work standing up, or they have to face the window or not face the window, or they can work only on a particular weight of typing paper, or they have to have a freshly brewed jug of coffee at hand. Some of them have a daily quota of a thousand words or so; others may write a sentence one day and a ream the next. What they all have in common is that they have to get down to it.

Getting down to it simply means starting at

the top left-hand corner of a page and going on until you reach the bottom right-hand corner, then repeating the process. Do not rush it, even when the ideas are flowing freely. If your brain is racing ahead of you, then write scribbled reminders to yourself. Whether you write in longhand or on a machine, always keep a scribbling pad at hand for notes, phrases that occur to you before your narrative is ready for them, and rough drafts of tricky sentences.

The journey from top to bottom of the page may be hard or it may be relatively smooth; it will almost certainly not be achieved without some obstacles in the way. These should be dealt with as they arise. Word-by-word correcting and line-by-line editing are an integral part of the writing process. It may be tedious: some of the liveliest writing is hacked out of tedium. In George Gissing's novel about Victorian literary drudgery, *New Grub Street*, perhaps the most detailed examination of the writer's trade ever published, there is a revealing account of the protagonist's struggle to fulfil his daily quota:

Sometimes the three hours' labour of a morning resulted in half a dozen lines, corrected into illegibility. His brain would not work; he could not recall the simplest synonyms; intolerable faults of composition drove him mad. He would write a sentence beginning thus: 'She took a book with the look of – ;' or thus: 'A revision of this decision would have made him an object of

> *derision.' Or, if the period were otherwise in-*
> *offensive, it ran in a rhythmic gallop which was*
> *torment to the ear.*

Note that he is using his ear. Despite a crippling obligation to churn out a three-volume novel of 200,000 words or so in forty-five days, Gissing's wretched hero cannot move on until he has eradicated the unwanted homophonic echoes of *took, book* and *look*, and *revision, decision, derision*, to which his writer's ear had alerted him.

Most writers are familiar with the torment of being unable to call to mind an elusive word. (Indeed, were the thought processes that led to the preceding sentence to be set down, they would read like an extract from *Roget's Thesaurus: Most writers are familiar with the sensation experience problem Tantalus grapes infuriating elusiveness elusive property torment* . . .) They know, too, the momentary panic induced by the brain's refusal to function, its sudden inability to frame the simplest of sentences. These minor outbreaks of writers' block are best remedied by driving on, setting down gibberish if necessary, and coming back to the problem later (Gissing's New Grub Street drudge could not afford the luxury of a second draft) when as often as not a solution will instantly recommend itself to the refreshed mind.

Unless actually paralysed by the word that will not come or the sentence that will not form itself, however, it is better to handle each stumbling-block as it comes along, getting each line right, listening for it to ring true, and then edging forward like a tunneller.

Re-drafting

One of the differences between the professional and the amateur writer is that the professional rarely believes he has got it right the first time. The amateur doesn't get it right either – but as likely as not he is satisfied with his first draft.

Rewriting does not come easily to a great many people, for the reason that they were never educated to it. Until comparatively recently, children could write up to a quarter of a million words in the course of their school careers and never be required to correct a line, except by way of imposition. Happily, one of the positive aspects of the new education is that pupils are nowadays encouraged to edit and re-edit their work after discussion and analysis, a task to which they take eagerly now that it can be accomplished on the word processor. It is in re-drafting in later life, incidentally, that the word processor comes into its own.

When re-drafting either a whole piece of work or a substantial section of it (an undertaking which many professionals will routinely and cheerfully repeat up to six times or more), you will be looking at the overall structure and feel of what you have written. Does it make sense? Is the material in the right order, or could it usefully do with some reshuffling? Above all, does it say what it set out to say, and in the tone of voice in which you meant to say it?

From this bird's-eye view you should then switch to a worm's-eye view, making a close line-by-line inspection. These are some of the so far undetected flaws to look out for:

Repetition: not only the same or similar-sounding words in the same sentence, but in too close proximity, for example, successive paragraphs opening with *Moreover*. (Material composed on the word processor, where it is gliding off the screen as you write, is vulnerable to this blemish.) Of course, it by no means necessarily follows (see 'Seven Deadly Sins': Elegant Variation) that each and every repeated word ought to be corrected: better a repetition than a strained synonym. It may also (see 'Sing As We Go': Hyperbole) be used for effect. Where it really should be corrected is where the same word crops up in the same sentence with different meanings: *As the train drew out, he wondered how he could train his nephew to be more punctual.*

Punctuation: even if your revision is only on a par with Oscar Wilde's 'In the morning I removed a comma; in the afternoon I put it back again', it is worth checking your stops thoroughly. Misplaced stops have a habit of creeping into the system; a pamphlet addressed to teenagers on the dangers of life got into print with this advice uncorrected: *When confronted with indecent exposure, don't stand frozen, walk away or criticize aloud.* The second comma replaced by a semicolon or dash might have saved an adolescent trauma.

Sentence construction: occasionally sentences which seemed perfectly sound when set down and re-read can suddenly read oddly. *Along with Mrs Jones, Mr Smith, Mr and Mrs Brown and their daughter, Mrs Black, who has been elected this year's secretary, was present at the meeting.* The sentence can perfectly well be read as it was meant to be read – Mrs Jones and Co. were at the meeting with Mrs Black who is this year's secretary. But, as with one of those trick pictures where a re-focus of the eye can throw up an altogether different image, it is easily possible to take it that Mrs Black is the Browns' daughter, and so subsequently flounder when the sentence appears to end prematurely. (It was a bad sentence anyway.)

Paragraphing: could your paragraphs do with being broken up a little to make the text look less daunting? Conversely, have you anywhere started a new paragraph, for the sake of taking a break, where the sense demands that the text should run on?

Simple slips: words omitted (very common), grammatical errors, literary lapses (for example, *on a lighter vein*, an absent-minded amalgam of *on a lighter note* and *in a lighter vein*), misspellings. We all have our own black dictionary of words which stubbornly refuse to be spelled correctly. It is a good idea not only to check on suspected misspellings but to check up, from time to time, on words we have always thought we have got right.

Second-best words: if there are any unsatisfactory words that you have set down because you just could not think of a better one, now is the time to browse through your vocabulary.

Sing As We Go

Listen analytically to any piece of music and you will find that irrespective of its merits, its composer has called upon a whole range of established techniques – balance and distribution of phrases, repetition, variations, rhythmic modes and so on – to flesh out and develop what, no matter how complex the work, could be reduced to a simple one-finger exercise. So it is with the written word. Without mastery of any of the techniques of his craft save succinctness, Shakespeare might have written *Sherry sharpens the tongue and warms the blood*. Instead, calling upon all the tricks of his trade, he wrote:

> *A good sherris-sack hath a two-fold operation in it. It ascends me into the brain; dries me there all the foolish and dull and crudy vapours which environ it; makes it apprehensive, quick, forgetive, full of nimble, fiery, and delectable shapes; which, deliver'd o'er to the voice, the tongue, which is the birth, becomes excellent*

wit. The second property of your excellent sherris is the warming of the blood; which before, cold and settled, left the liver white and pale, which is the badge of pusillanimity and cowardice; but the sherris warms it and makes it course from the inwards to the parts' extreme. It illumineth the face, which, as a beacon, gives warning to all the rest of this little kingdom, man, to arm; and then the vital commoners, and inland petty spirits, muster me all to their captain, the heart, who, great and puffed up with this retinue, doth any deed of courage; and this valour comes of sherris. So that skill in the weapon is nothing without sack, for that sets it a-work; and learning a mere hoard of gold kept by a devil, till sack commences it and sets it in act and use.

The techniques that go into making the language sing are the instruments in the writer's orchestra. Most of the following, and more, were brought into play in that passage from *Henry IV*, Part II.

Metaphor

Metaphor, not to be confused with *simile* (see below) is where we take words out of one sphere and apply them to another: *In opposing this Bill the Hon. Member is swimming against the tide*. Metaphor may be either a phrase (The Government may as well *shut up shop*; I was *sold a pup*; we have been *led up a blind alley*) or a single word (*scuppered* his plans; *throttle* the economy; *marry* the two resolutions). The idea of metaphor, like the idea of simile, is to enliven one's narrative with vivid imagery, like Shakespeare's *the face, which as a beacon* (simile), *gives warning to all the rest of this little kingdom, man* (metaphor). Unfortunately it often has the reverse effect.

Much of the language we use is metaphorical in origin. When you have a *view* on some issue or other you are using a metaphor borrowed from sight. It follows that if you have *outspoken views*, you are literally speaking what you see. The absurdity does not matter, however, since this is what linguists call *dead metaphor*, which means that the metaphorical connection with a word's original meaning has passed into the corporate unconscious. And so, whether we realize it or not, metaphor accounts for a great part, perhaps even the greater part, of our vocabulary.

Dead metaphor is a far cry from outworn metaphor: *kick against the pricks, put all your eggs in one basket, take the bull by the horns.* These and a thousand other metaphors have been so over-used that we are often hard put to frame the unmetaphorical phrases they are standing in for. How do you say *Why take coals to Newcastle?* to convey your literal meaning? It is a struggle, but worth it: if what you are really saying is, for example, *Why are you packing apples when we are having our picnic in an orchard?*, the factual imagery is far more graphic than the fanciful. *That's all in the past* has more force than the sluggish *water under the bridge.*

Then there is metaphor so familiar (*run with the fox, count your chickens, the last straw*) that it does not even have to be completed – in which case it is probably better not started. But sometimes, once started, it has to be finished. You can say *This was the last straw: it led to his dismissal*, since the last straw metaphor is rarely spelled out these days. What you cannot say is *This was the last straw that led to his dismissal*. Once the last straw's relative pronoun *that* has been brought into it, there is no going back, and you have to plod on to the end of a well-worn path: *This was the last straw that broke the camel's back: it led to his dismissal*. The journey was hardly worth embarking upon.

Unsustained metaphor is another familiar pitfall: *If he thinks the public will support this measure then he is burying his head in the sand* does not sustain its metaphor. To bury one's head in the sand is to delude oneself by wilfully ignoring certain facts or figures. Merely having an opinion about the public's support for a measure may involve a certain amount of self-delusion, but not to the degree called for by the ostrich parallel. Metaphor may be wildly extravagant but it has to be justified.

Inappropriate metaphor is very common: *By making light of this matter we are whistling in the dark . . . Placing your bet before you know the form is putting the cart before the horse . . . If the postman doesn't lodge a complaint about being bitten, I think we should let sleeping dogs lie . . . By* its very nature, metaphor should be far removed from the subject at hand.

And so to mixed metaphor. *It's like a game of chess: all the cards are thrown in the air, the board's turned over, and you're in a completely different ball game.* An extreme example, perhaps, but mixed metaphor is common enough: *took the wind out of his sails and left him with egg on his face . . . He thought he would take the bull by the horns but instead he shot himself through the foot . . . We are sitting on a time-bomb yet we fiddle while Rome burns . . .* There the mixing of metaphors is obvious and not difficult to be on the alert for, especially if one avoids worn-out metaphor in the first place. It is easy, however, to fall into unconscious mixed metaphor: *This paves the way to giving him a stranglehold on the entire industry* (*stranglehold* may be well on the way to becoming dead metaphor by now, but laying down a pavement to the wrestling ring nevertheless seems, meanwhile, a bizarre activity); *Taking a bird's-eye view of the situation, I'd say we were up the creek without a paddle* (we cannot be up in the air and in a canoe simultaneously); *We're working against the clock but I'm afraid the sands are rapidly running out* (of the clock?). The surest safeguard against mixed metaphor is to put it to the test by applying it literally. When you find yourself unable to picture someone pulling up a ladder while sitting in a lifeboat, then you know something is wrong.

Do not confuse mixed metaphor with

changed metaphor. *We are in hock up to our armpits* and *He is hand in glove with a self-confessed Judas* are not mixed metaphor but changed metaphor, as is *This royal throne of kings, this sceptred isle,/ This earth of majesty* etc. The only charge against changed metaphor is that, as may be seen from those examples, it may somewhat over-egg the pudding.

Overdone metaphor, of the kind used by politicians with their *touches on the tiller, rocky shores, calmer waters* and so forth, is both tedious and time-wasting, its main function being to disguise the speaker's inability to come up with anything original to say. We cannot do without metaphor – try thinking up a more concise definition than *a chicken and egg situation* – but, as with all other forms of expression, the original is to be preferred over the familiar, provided that the original says it better. There will always be a place for striking, usually topical, invented metaphor: *The Prime Minister's flying pickets; Rottweiler politics; not only changing the goalposts but nobbling the referee.*

Simile

A simile is a direct comparison of one thing with another: *as silent as the grave, as good as gold, as free as air.* The comparison has to be stated rather than implied, usually with the help of a conjunction, otherwise it is probably a metaphor. *He's crazy like a fox* is simile. *He's a wolf in sheep's clothing* is metaphor.

As the examples already quoted show,

there is much overworked simile in circulation: Eric Partridge lists three columns of what he calls 'battered similes' in his *Usage and Abusage*, among them *clean as a whistle, drunk as a lord, sober as a judge, slippery as an eel, keen as mustard* . . . Many of our modern street-language similes, though equally overexposed, remain more fresh and colourful than the old chestnuts: *bent as a fiddler's elbow, thick as two short planks, sick as a parrot*.

Simile is easy to invent because it is nearly always simple in form (although it does not have to be: *as hard to ignore as a vacuum cleaner*); but because it is easy to invent it is easy to overdo. Dylan Thomas's *My tongue is as hot as a camel-saddle mounted by baked Bedouins* overdoes it. So do similes delivered in clusters: *It was as hot as a baker's oven. The air was as thick as soup and as steamy as a swamp, and the tropical orchids in bloom smelled as overpowering as a perfume factory*. . . This is of course the impurest sub-Chandlerese. Let us look at the real piece of Chandler from which it was corrupted: 'Then it was really hot. The air was thick, wet, steamy and larded with the cloying smell of tropical orchids in bloom . . .' Not a simile in sight – until he finds the right opportunity for one, when he delivers a classic: 'They smelled as overpowering as boiling alcohol under a blanket.'

Comparison

Comparison, a blood relative of simile, is the art of likening one thing to another, usually in a surrealist, hyperbolic way, for the sake of illustration.

English is rich in striking comparison, the masters being Shakespeare (*Like snail unwillingly to school*), Wodehouse (*Like a bishop who had just discovered Schism and Doubt among the minor clergy*) and Chandler (*A slanting grey rain like a swung curtain of crystal beads*). There are also many anonymous masters of the form: *fits like a shirt on a wheelbarrow; like a tart in a trance; a face like the back of a bus-smash.*

Like *hyperbole* (see below), comparison can easily overstep the mark. *Like a dog that has won an extra tail in a raffle* is an effort to get away from the stock *Like a dog with two tails.* Unfortunately it does not get far enough away, and the comparison compares badly with Wodehouse.

The dog with two tails leads us to cliché. Like every other form of imagery, comparison has its knacker's yard of cliché: *Like a bat out of hell . . . a bear with a sore head . . . ton of bricks . . . two peas in a pod . . . gold dust . . . nothing on earth . . . a giant refreshed . . . a man possessed . . . the curate's egg . . .* Without going to the lengths of the dog that won its extra tail in a raffle, you do not have to be a Wodehouse or a Chandler to replace an outworn comparison with a fresh one.

Taking *like a bat out of hell* as an example, let us see how a comparison is constructed. The first thing to consider is what we would be saying if we had to be literal, without the aid of imagery; and what we would be saying is probably something on the lines of *He was off as fast as I have seen anyone run*. This is where we see the uses of figurative comparison, for the literal comparison of *as fast as* etc. does not catch that impression of impetus that we want to put over. So it is an analogy for *impetus* we are looking for: something that sets off, or better still is released, at high speed. The need for such a comparison at once liberates the imagination and constrains it. *He was off like a rabbit out of a hat* suggests impetus but not speed: we do not think of the rabbit making off once it has emerged from the hat. *He was off like a jet off a runway* has speed but not impetus: it does not have that feeling of release or escape after being held back that we get from *a bat out of hell*. *He was off like a rocket* is better, but it has thrust rather than impetus in the sense we are looking for. *He was off like a greyhound out of a trap* suits our purpose, but while it is not so much of a cliché as the bat out of hell, it is still a fairly well-worn phrase. *He was off like a rat up a drainpipe* is familiar yet expressive, but it is still not quite what we want. But the thought process does lead us to *He was off like a cat out of the oven*. What the cat was doing in the oven we do not know, but the image seems to do the trick.

Comparisons are fun to invent, and always add colour to a narrative so long as they are not laboured or absurdly overstated. The secret is not to let the comparison outshine what is being described. Dorothy Parker's *handwriting like the lesser rivers on maps* evokes a picture of spidery handwriting. D.H. Lawrence's *a laugh like a blackbird in a bush* evokes a picture of a blackbird.

Note that phrases such as *like there was no tomorrow, like he had a rocket up his backside* and *like he hadn't had a drink for a month* are not comparisons, neither are they English. They are American idiomatic expressions, and to anglicize them we should change each *like* to *as if*.

Hyperbole

Hyperbole is the use of (usually) gross exaggeration for emphasis: *I'd walk a million miles for one of your smiles*. It is often used for humorous effect: *It was the height of the tourist season, and in Trafalgar Square half the population of Tokyo were taking photographs of the other half*. It may also be used poetically, when it is an advantage to be Shakespeare: *I'll put a girdle round about the earth*.

In good hands (*a diamond as big as the Ritz*) hyperbole has the desired effect. In less expert hands (*I was hanging on the phone for hours*) it sounds lacklustre and lazy, the more so since much hyperbole has been re-cycled into cliché (*They were swinging from the chandeliers . . . I could eat a horse . . . he's got money coming out of his ears*).

Nothing is worse (to use an everyday example of hyperbole) than strained hyperbole: *a coal tip the size of a small mountain* evokes the desired image of largeness; *a coal tip the size of Mount Everest* merely sounds far-fetched. Paradoxically, it is all too easy for hyperbole to over-exaggerate, and that is where inexperienced writers come unstuck. Wodehouse can get away with it – *He's as jealous as billy-ho. Smear a bit of burnt cork on him, and he could step right on to any stage and play Othello without rehearsal* – but lesser talents often find themselves floundering: *He's such a bad shot he couldn't hit Jodrell Bank at close range*. This is very poor: the writer presumably has in mind Jodrell Bank radio telescope, which he has selected because it is not only huge but round, the shape of a rifle target. But the image doesn't work – it is too remote and too preposterous. *He's such a bad shot he couldn't hit a dinner plate at close range* would diminish the degree of exaggeration by about 25,000 per cent yet at the same time sharpen it.

The best hyperbole has a twist to it, boosting but not overdoing the exaggeration. *Had I but one penny left in the world, it would be yours* makes its point all right, but the sentence rather limps home. See what it becomes in Shakespeare's hands: *An I had but one penny in the world, thou shouldst have it to buy gingerbread*. The strength is doubled.

However, sustained hyperbole, where one image after another is piled on to heighten the exaggeration, rarely works. *Uncle Charlie got so legless at the wedding they had to push him home in a wheelbarrow – he had champagne coming out of his ears* is, to use the opposite of hyperbole which is understatement, over-doing it a little.

Never allow the expression *literally* anywhere near a piece of hyperbole. *They were literally at it hammer and tongs* means that a hammer and a pair of tongs were being used as offensive weapons. *Literally* literally means *literally*.

Rhetoric

Rhetoric, the art of persuasive eloquence, has an unsavoury reputation, associated as it is with political windbaggery and evangelical tub-thumping. Indeed, it is rarely these days that one sees the word unaccompanied by the adjective 'empty'. Yet rhetoric, properly used, is a powerful weapon in the writer's armoury. Nor does it have to be self-indulgent or overblown – rhetoric can just as effectively be skilful in its understatement. Thus Bernard Levin on a young woman shot by East German border guards: 'She was murdered because she wanted to change her address.'

Repetition in one form or another is perhaps the most used rhetorical device, a celebrated example being Martin Luther King's 'I have a dream' speech. The repetition may be of a word or group of words or of an idea. 'Sans teeth, sans eyes, sans taste, sans everything' is rhetorical repetition, as is Neil Kinnock's injunction to voters in the event of his electoral defeat: 'I warn you not to be ordinary, I warn you not to be young, I warn you not to fall ill, I warn you not to get old.' Politicians are extremely fond of this form of rhetorical utterance, from the Churchillian 'We shall fight on the beaches, we shall fight on the landing grounds, we shall fight in the fields and in the streets, we shall fight in the hills, we shall never surrender' to the more mundane back-bencher's 'We do care about jobs, we do care about education, we do care about the nation's health . . .' Repetition in this instance is not the same as repetitiousness – see how bald rhetorical prose looks when stripped of its repetitions: *We shall fight on the beaches, on the landing grounds, and in the fields, streets and hills . . . I warn you not to be ordinary or young, and not to fall ill or get old.* Even *I warn you not to be ordinary, not to be young, not to fall ill, not to get old*, while retaining the rhetorical form, loses much of the power of the original.

While only one of the examples quoted here follows the principle, the rule of three is a safe one to follow with rhetorical repetition. Churchill could get away with a series of four, but beyond that you are in danger of being merely repetitive without the rhetoric. Very effective, in contrast to this tuppence-coloured phraseology, is the penny-plain singular repetition: 'I say this without malice and without rancour . . .' Compare: *I say this without malice or rancour.*

Wordplay is another strong element of rhetoric. Again Churchill: 'This is not the end. It is not even the beginning of the end.

But it is, perhaps, the end of the beginning' – an altogether more dramatic and telling way of putting it than *This is the beginning of the middle*. Rhetoric is probably the only area of composition where letting several words do the work of one may be justified – if they are words that make their mark. Abraham Lincoln could have said *Eighty-seven years ago* instead of 'Fourscore and seven years ago', but to less effect.

Repetition is sometimes allied with alliteration. As Shaw has Professor Higgins remark about Alfred Doolittle, 'This chap has a certain natural gift of rhetoric. Observe the rhythm of his native woodnotes wild. "I'm willing to tell you; I'm wanting to tell you; I'm waiting to tell you." ' But apt alliteration's artful aid is a rhetorical device best handled with care by the inexperienced writer. Alliteration is something more than a string of words starting with the same letter or with the same sound, as in *Veni, vidi, vici, Wills' Wild Woodbines* or the headline writer's *Leggy Lovely Lands Up Legless*. It is, in skilful hands, the art of establishing the rhythm of a sentence by pointing up words so that they beckon one to another like sea beacons. G.K. Chesterton is the acknowledged master of alliteration: 'When fishes flew and forests walked/ And figs grew upon thorn,/ Some moment when the moon was blood/ Then surely I was born. . .' (see also *Rhythm* below). Not to be commended is alliteration for humorous effect, the end result of which nearly always turns out like something out of *Comic Cuts*: *The priceless pair were in a pickle* ... Unconscious alliteration (*When William walked in, we all wondered what he would say*) should of course be corrected, and always is corrected by writers who are in the habit of listening to their own words as they set them down.

Rhetoric has to be worthy of the occasion: Lincoln would not have written to his landlord *I paid the rent three and twenty days ago*. And it must not degenerate into purple prose. When you have indulged yourself in a rhetorical passage, read it out loud (rhetoric is really meant to be spoken rather than written), and if it makes you blush, scrap it.

Idiom

Idiom is that vast storehouse of expressions in common – and uncommon – use which may well be ungrammatical, which may not even make sense when looked at in isolation, yet which add immeasurably to the English language. Idiom is an understanding of what our language is all about: when we say *Could I have a word?* it is understood that we mean *Could I have a few words?* or even, according to the tone used, *Could I have very many words?*

There are so many idiomatic expressions, in so many loose categories, that it is but the work of a few moments to compose an alphabet of typical idioms: *armed to the teeth, bite the dust, caught with his pants down, dead to the world, end of one's tether, flash in the pan, give a wide berth to, hard and fast, in the soup, join issue, kick over the traces, let the cat out of the bag, make do and mend, neither here nor there, out of the wood, pull one's weight, queer one's pitch, run the gauntlet, screw up one's courage, two-faced, under the weather, vicious circle, walk on air, year in year out, zero hour.* Idiom draws its inspiration from an astonishing variety of sources. The above list takes its references from the army, the navy and the air force; from the legal and sporting worlds; from horsemanship; from the fairground and from seventeenth-century firearms; and from a variety of expressions which have simply wandered into the language in the most casual way. While at least one of the foregoing may be attributed to Shakespeare (Partridge tells us that *screw up one's courage* is a corruption of *Screw your courage to the sticking-place* – *Macbeth*), and while many of our idioms are truncated quotations (*sly dog, perish the thought, will never hold water* – not Shakespeare but the now-forgotten Colley Cibber 1671–1757), it is a quality of idiom that as often as not has its origins in the spoken rather than the written word. Idiom is truly the voice of the people.

It will be seen that all the examples quoted could equally be classified as clichés. Yet idioms have far more staying power than clichés. If you heard the phrase *He couldn't say boo to a goose* half a dozen times in a week you would probably groan and wonder why someone couldn't think of a more original way of saying the same thing. But if you heard *make no mistake* or *went off at half-cock* or *roll up one's sleeves* six times in the same week the repetition would probably not even register. We do sometimes like to vary our idioms a little – we might choose to say *caught with his trousers round his ankles, at the end of one's rope, in the jolly old consommé* – but in the main they do not grate no matter how many times we hear them. We have something of the affection for idioms that we have for old hymn tunes; and it is a source of the keenest pleasure to know that our idioms often puzzle foreigners (language, despite its polyglot nature, is the first refuge of the patriot: hence the Académie française, hence the Walloon riots, hence similar disturbances on the Indian sub-continent and within the USSR). How are they to know the difference between the wrong horse, the horse of a different colour, the horse that one should not change in mid-stream, the gift horse, the stalking horse, the Trojan horse, the high horse, the horse that one puts the cart before, the hobby horse, and the horse that one locks the stable door behind after it has bolted?

Besides ready-made idioms there is the idiomatic use of language where it is understood that while what we are saying is ungrammatical or illogical or both, everyone knows what we are talking about: *The Prince arrived alone, with the Princess expected later.* Since the Prince is not with the Princess but without her, this makes no sense; yet we allow it, just as we allow *to close down* to mean almost the same, yet subtly not the same, as *to close up*; and as we can say *I shouldn't be surprised if he didn't turn up*, which when you cancel out the double negatives does not mean the same as *I should be surprised if he did turn up*; and as we know the difference in meaning between *Now now!* and *Now then!*, both of which exclamations on the face of it say nothing at all. We say *steam-rollered* when logic demands *steam-rolled*; and we even speak idiomatically, although perhaps we shouldn't, of *the height of the Depression*.

We sprinkle our language with idioms as we sprinkle our food with salt and pepper, and for the same reason: to bring out the flavour. Much communication would be bland and tasteless without the tang of idiom: compare *You can drop that tone of voice at once* with *You can drop that tone of voice for a kick-off*. Idioms only become tedious where they plod hand in hand into the mire of mixed metaphor: *At an educated guess, even if you had the guts to go out on a limb and move heaven and earth to put the kybosh on his little game, you could end up with egg on your face*.

Far more fruitful than stringing used idioms together like worry beads is inventing new idioms. If you say that someone is *not all there* you are using established idiom; if you say they are *one sandwich short of a picnic* you are using invented idiom. Like comparison, idiom is amusing to invent, and once again Chandler and Wodehouse are our role models: *A blonde to make a bishop kick a hole in a stained-glass window . . . A city with all the personality of a paper cup . . . She gave me a smile I could feel in my hip pocket* (Chandler); *The sort of eye that can open an oyster at sixty paces . . . I gave Motty the swift east-to-west . . . Fate was quietly slipping the lead into the boxing glove* (Wodehouse). Often something of a cross between hyperbole and simile, invented idiom, in the right place, can be an enlivening influence on an otherwise pedestrian narrative.

Quotation

'It is a good thing for an uneducated man to read books of quotations' said Sir Winston Churchill – in a book of quotations. In fact whatever the standard of our education and whether we read books of quotations or not, all but the most intellectually impoverished of us have an enormous repertoire of quotations, including the nursery rhymes of our childhood, fragments of poetry and lines of Shakespeare remembered from school, the pop songs we grew up with, catchphrases from radio and television shows, political and advertising slogans, odd lines from books and newspaper articles that for one reason or another have stuck in the memory, and a host of popular sayings coined by no one knows who (*Changing the deckchairs on the Titanic . . . You don't get many of those to the pound . . . It'll all be the same in a hundred years' time*).

The best-known quotations should be the ones least quoted by any self-respecting writer. Quotations degenerate in the fulness of time into clichés, and there is no more mileage to be got out of *Letting I dare not wait upon I would* except in a performance of *Macbeth*. The same goes for the poor cat.

But quotation can be, and should be, of immense benefit to the writer. Any quotation that provides an insight into what you are writing about, or that says something better than you can say it yourself, or that illustrates a point, has earned the space it occupies.

There are one or two cautions to keep in mind. Ensure that the quotation means what you think it means, by going to the original context if necessary. *Thirty pieces of silver* refers to betrayal, not bribery. Get the quotation right, again by checking. *A little learning* (not *a little knowledge*) *is a dang'rous thing. Comparisons are odorous*, not *odious*.

Do not drag quotations in by the heels. If they appear to intrude or to interrupt your narrative, cross them out. Cross them out the more ferociously if you have only introduced them to air your knowledge.

Tampering with quotations to create an elaborate piece of metaphor is generally foolhardy: *In providing for too many health and safety cooks with powers of inspection, the Government will be in danger of spoiling the broth of free enterprise* commits the double offence of introducing an over-familiar quotation and then subjecting it to creaking adaptation. This is not to say that quotations may not occasionally be tinkered with to amusing effect: *There but for the grace of God goes God . . . I think that I shall never see/ A billboard lovely as a tree.*

Quotations may often be editorialized, that is, used without quotation marks and adapted to the tense and mood of the borrower's narrative: *We all knew that a little learning was a dangerous thing* rather than *We all knew that 'a little learning is a dang'rous thing'*. Nor is there any need, at least with the better-known quotations, to acknowledge authorship or source: *We all knew that, as Alexander Pope put it in his* Essay on Criticism, *a little learning* etc. would be tedious. Lesser-known or unfamiliar quotations should be attributed briefly and unobtrusively: *Time wounds all heels, as Groucho said.*

Unless you are writing in French, find an English equivalent for any French quotation you may be tempted to introduce to your readers.

Punctuation

We have already considered the uses of the various stops. What we have not considered is punctuation as an aid to style.

While punctuation's first function is to clarify what otherwise could be obscure or downright misleading (note, for example, how leaving the comma out of *However, we may look at the proposals again* misleads the reader: *However we may look at the proposals . . .*), it also has the important task of controlling the flow of words, acting here as a dam, there as a conduit.

Look at two closely adjacent passages in a story by W.W. Jacobs:

> *Lawyer Quince, so called by his neighbours in Little Haven from his readiness at all times to place at their disposal the legal lore he had acquired from a few old books while following his useful occupation of making boots, sat in a kind of wooden hutch at the side of his cottage plying his trade ... Heavy footsteps and the sound of voices raised in dispute caused him to look up from his work. Mr Rose, of Holly Farm, Hogg, the miller, and one or two neighbours of lesser degree appeared to be in earnest debate over some point of unusual difficulty.*

In the first sentence, parenthetical commas channel the thirty-eight words of its subordinate clause so that they sail effortlessly along their tributary, re-connecting with the mainstream without difficulty. In the second sentence it is the very absence of commas that helps the words on their way. In the third sentence, apparently needless commas (after *Rose* and *Hogg*) act as brakes to vary the speed of the sentence in contrast to the smooth pace of the passage it follows.

See how less discriminating attention to punctuation could have affected this extract:

> *Lawyer Quince, so called by his neighbours in Little Haven from his readiness, at all times, to place at their disposal the legal lore he had*

acquired from a few old books, while following
his useful occupation of making boots, sat in a
kind of wooden hutch at the side of his cottage,
plying his trade . . . Heavy footsteps, and the
sound of voices raised in dispute, caused him to
look up from his work. Mr Rose of Holly Farm,
Hogg the miller, and one or two neighbours of
lesser degree, appeared to be in earnest debate
over some point of unusual difficulty.

Every addition or deletion of a comma
could be justified, yet the flow of the passage
is ruined.

Use punctuation not only as a pause maker
but as a pacemaker.

Rhythm

We have touched on rhythm under several
headings in this manual. It is worth a few
words more to sum up this section.

Rhythm is to language as it is to music: it is
the beat, the flow, and only the ear can tell
you whether the rhythm is there or not. A
piece of writing without rhythm reads like
the small print in an Act of Parliament. A
piece of writing with the wrong rhythm reads
as if one were trying to read it in a badly
sprung stagecoach. A piece of writing with
the rhythm just so is a joy to read.

Rhythm does not mean fancy rhythm; you
are not trying to make your prose sound like
poetry (although if you were, there is no
better model than the Song of Solomon in the
Authorized Version, and no worse one than

the same chapters in any of the new versions). Rhythm is achieving the desired effect by as many controls as there are stops on an organ: punctuation, repetition, alliteration, the juxtaposition of one word with another – of a long word with a short one, or two long ones and a short one, or several short words together; the insertion of a relative clause of a particular length, the inversion of a phrase, and so on. See how all the controls mentioned here have shaped the opening lines of a short story by G.K. Chesterton:

> *There was a brief period during which Father Brown enjoyed, or rather did not enjoy, something like fame. He was a nine days' wonder in the newspapers; he was even a common topic of controversy in the weekly reviews; his exploits were narrated eagerly and inaccurately in any number of clubs and drawing rooms, especially in America. Incongruous and indeed incredible as it may seem to anyone who knew him, his adventures as a detective were even made the subject of short stories appearing in magazines.*

A piece of writing without rhythm is like a load of sand being tipped out of a lorry. The goods ordered have been delivered, but with no thought of finesse and no effort to regulate their despatch. Rhythmless writing speaks in a monotone. Rhythmical writing is the sound of words singing.

Seven Deadly Sins

Good writing consists in large part of avoiding certain mannerisms of style which, like most bad habits, are easy enough to throw off once one has become aware of how and why they offend. The most common ones, over and above the jarring rhythms summarized in 'The Tin Ear', are given here.

Cliché

A cliché is an over-used phrase which, if metaphorical, has lost its power to evoke even the feeblest image in the eye of the reader – *raining cats and dogs, upset the apple cart, gilding the lily*; or, if abstract, has lost the impact it once had – *infinite capacity for taking pains, new lease of life, neither rhyme nor reason*. Of course we all know what these phrases mean, but the zest has been squeezed out of them. Many of them were fresh only the day before yesterday: *elements of refurbishment, tired and emotional, economical with the truth*. Others are mummified relics of another age:

hoist by his own petard, lock, stock and barrel, shipshape and Bristol fashion. No matter that their origins may be lost: clichés are symbols, ideograms, expressing the idea of a thing without saying its name.

Although Sam Goldwyn advised us to avoid clichés like the plague, it is remarkably difficult to write for any length of time without resorting to cliché; nor (as the title of this section testifies) should one always try. When you say someone has *put the cat among the pigeons* you are talking shorthand, and your audience is likely to grasp your meaning more quickly and clearly than if you had worked hard at an original metaphor and come up with, say, *put the piranha among the goldfish,* which sounds embarrassingly forced. *At the eleventh hour* is old hat; yet it still carries more clout than *at the very last minute.* So some clichés are less deadly than others.

There are many kinds of cliché: the over-familiar quotation (*stood not upon the order of his going*); the hackneyed Latin tag (*mutatis mutandis*); the long-lost metaphor (*tilt at windmills*); the boring formula (*share and share alike*); the faded image (*sweep the board*); the utilitarian (*give chapter and verse*); the jargon-istic (*U-turn*); and so on. There is even the instantaneous – the phrase so sententious that it is a cliché the instant it is coined (*We live in a world where the flame of freedom is burning ever more brightly*). Single words may be clichés – *viable, situation, megabucks.* And still they come. Eric Partridge's *Dictionary of*

Clichés lists them by the hundred, yet it remains a hopelessly incomplete work in that as old clichés, like old soldiers, reluctantly fade away (cliché), new clichés queue up to take their place. *State of the art, no way, you must be joking* . . . In the fertile new breeding grounds of the mass media, clichés proliferate as never before.

Let us concede that when going singly about their business, clichés are capable of performing a service. It is when they huddle together like derelicts under a railway arch that the trouble starts:

> *The Great Wen was sleeping the sleep of the just, and I had only these mortal remains, which having looked on the wine when it was red had drunk not wisely but too well, as my friend in need. Silence reigned supreme at the hub of the Empire. A gilded youth of my acquaintance came out of a rubescent brick club as I passed. A wilting bloom drooped from his buttonhole; he had been playing with the devil's picture books, and was going home with the milk before the roseate dawn.*

The same passage in the hands of Rudyard Kipling:

> *All London was asleep, and I had only this drunken carcass to bear me company. It was silent – silent as chaste Piccadilly. A young man of my acquaintance came out of a pink brick club as I passed. A faded carnation drooped from his buttonhole; he has been*

playing cards, and was walking home before the dawn.

Clichés do have their uses, but the piece of work that can get by without their help is the better for it.

Wordiness

Verbosity is the enemy of good writing. An addiction to words, you might think, is the mark of the true craftsman. The reverse is generally true. The best writers regard words with the deepest suspicion, never introducing a newcomer to their vocabulary until it has shown what it can do that other words can't, and never admitting any word into their writing that cannot prove its worth.

A parliamentary draftsman apologized to his masters: 'I am sorry this letter is so long. If I had had time I could have made it shorter.' It is a sound principle to follow. Never use three words where two will do, nor two where one will do – especially if they say the same thing (*root cause, past history, important essentials*).

Cut out dead wood. *As to whether* and *as to why* can usually be reduced to *whether* and *why* (and *respectively* appended to this sentence would be a redundancy). *In view of the fact that* should be *since* or *because*. *Must* is a powerful word in its own right; it does not need to be accompanied by *inevitably*, *positively* or *necessarily*. *Definitely* should be declared a non-word. Phrases borrowed from officialese – *it should be appreciated, it will be recalled that, it is important to realize that* – should simply be crossed out.

Unless a subordinate clause seems worth a diversion, take the shortest route to the end of a sentence and do not pick up any extraneous words on the way. *Public service broadcasting should provide geographical universality of coverage* could have dumped its excessive baggage to become *Public service broadcasting should be available everywhere.* This example was cited in a House of Lords debate on English by Lord Airedale, who also quoted the memorial to William Pitt in the Guildhall which is inscribed 'He died poor' and not, as an alderman suggested as being more dignified, 'He expired in indigent circumstances.'

Avoid all circumlocutory language. Use simple prepositions: *about*, not *with regard to*; *because*, not *for the reason that*; *except*, not *with the exception of*; *besides*, not *in addition to*; *after*, not *subsequent to*.

Always use a word in its shortest appropriate form – *transport*, not *transportation*, *preventive*, not *preventative*, *medicine*, not *medicament* or *medication*. Where a shorter substitute exists, use it – *part*, not *proportion*, *take part*, not *participate*, *use*, not *utilization*. A caution, however: longer words are capable of more shades of meaning than many short words, and so the short, plain word cannot always express precisely what the longer word has to say for itself. *Demonstrate*, for example,

means much more than *show*: when you ask
for a free demonstration, you are asking for
something other than a free show. Then
again, longer words do not always mean
what shorter words take them to mean. *Enor-
mity* does not mean *size*, it means *the state of
being monstrous*. Check with the dictionary.

That being said, and allowing that an endless succession of short words can be as
wearying as a tramp across Salisbury Plain,
the Old English monosyllable is nearly
always more powerful than the Latin-based
polysyllable. See the first fifty words of
Genesis:

> *In the beginning God created the heaven and the
> earth. And the earth was without form, and
> void; and darkness was upon the face of the
> deep. And the Spirit of God moved upon the
> face of the waters. And God said, Let there be
> light: and there was light.*

All but five words are single syllables or
have single-syllable roots.

Jokiness
Joking with the reader is all very well if the
jokes are good and the occasion is appropriate. What might go down well at the annual
dinner may not go down well in the annual
report; and even at the annual dinner it will
not get its round of applause if the speaker
does not know how to put a joke over. In the
wrong hands, especially if they are heavy
hands, attempted humour can be excruciating.

Any would-be humorist who has even contemplated putting an exclamation mark in brackets (!) to signal a supposed witticism should leave the form to its professional practitioners. As for puns, Fowler is surprisingly tolerant of them on the basis that they may be good, bad or indifferent, 'and only those who lack the wit to make them are unaware of the fact'. The trouble is that those who lack the wit to make them are the ones who make them most. We only have to glance at the tabloid papers (*Eau no! water turn-off for Perrier!* etc.) to see where an addiction to punning can lead.

Besides the out-and-out attempted rib-tickler, other groan-inducing effects include *facetiousness, flippancy, jocularity, irony, heavy-handedness* and *joshery*.

Facetiousness is the compulsive determination to make even the most unpromising material amusing: *Despite all that, tea was required, and I was set to work to get it. I did! In fact, never have our fellows known so much tea-getting in all their existence as I treated them to on that Sabbath afternoon.* (The example is from an Edwardian piece of holiday reading a long way after Jerome K. Jerome. While the style has dated, the technique remains as deeply embedded in aspic as ever.)

Flippancy is the inability to speak seriously even when the occasion demands it: *Now that Max Wall has gone to the great Palladium in the sky and Tommy Trinder has slipped on the banana skin of life, who is there left?* The writer, unfortunately.

Jocularity is the infuriating habit of clouding every issue with a jest: *We come now to our treasurer's impending resignation; or to put it another way we do not come now to our treasurer's impending resignation, since he is yet to come to it himself.* Is the man about to resign or not?

Irony is the use of words to suggest their opposite: *The effect of all-day opening of licensed premises, I do not doubt, would be to turn heavy drinkers into moderate drinkers and moderate drinkers into teetotallers.* A dangerous weapon – H.L. Mencken proposed a typeface to be called ironics, sloping the opposite way from italics, to show that what was being said was not to be taken literally. The trouble is that the more obvious the irony, the less effective it is, while sustained irony is an embarrassment to the reader.

Heavy-handedness is the pedant at play. His playthings are hoary old comical clichés (*the cup that cheers, the trouble and strife, as the bishop said to the actress*), borrowed catchphrases (*titter ye not, how does that affect the price of fish?*), laboured ellipses (*he was short of breath, cash and temper*), ponderous polysyllables (*pedestrian extremities*) and the like. As he would himself say, *'Nuff said.*

Joshery is the kind of non-stop babble you get in oral form from saloon bar lives and souls of the party. It comes freely bespattered with exclamation marks and brackets: *Well well well, look who it isn't!!! Yes, friends (and foes?? Only pulling your proverbial, Dave), behind that red plastic conk lurks none other than our one and only Sales Rep of the Year Dave the Rave! (Surprise surprise!)* The fact that perpetrations of this sort are usually for private circulation barely lessens the anguish.

None of this is to discourage a lightness of touch in almost any field of writing. The writer who can pen a technical report, say, in an easy, conversational style has a talent his colleagues should envy.

Elegant variation

Elegant variation – which in many instances would be better styled inelegant variation – is the practice of reaching for a strained synonym for fear of repeating oneself; for example, *The dog pursued the cat at high speed through the French windows – but it was the hound that returned with its tail between its legs.* There are worse examples, as when a ball becomes a *sphere*, a horse becomes a *steed*, a pub landlord *mine host*, the Queen *the monarch*, or an inhabitant a *denizen*. Some writers of dialogue are terrified of repeating *said*, so that on any given page only one of their characters is allowed to say, while the rest *aver*, *pronounce*, *declare*, *exclaim*, *reply*, *interrupt*, *retort*, *interject* and *assert*. Tabloid

133

journalists especially have a fondness for *stuff* as a universal synonym: *Britain is eating more chocolate than ever. In ten years we have more than doubled our intake of the stuff* . . . You may be sure, too, that *eating* will make but one appearance in such a report: thereafter Britain will be *chomping, sinking its teeth into, chewing its way through* etc.

English is rich in synonyms – we have *Roget's Thesaurus* stuffed full of them – and so it should not be difficult, as a rule, to find an acceptable alternative to a word already used. The art is in not choosing a pedantic synonym (*feathered friends* for birds, *libation* for drink), or a laboured one (*abode* for home, *apparatus* for telephone). But we have to accept that some words just do not have adequate synonyms. A rose is a rose is a rose: it is not, at least in variation of itself, a bloom, nosegay or buttonhole. If a word bears repetition, then repeat it: there is nothing wrong with *The rose garden was in full bloom, the roses at their best*.

Of course it is not always a good idea to give the same word two airings in a single sentence, or for that matter even in adjoining ones. *The dog pursued the cat at high speed through the French windows – but it was the dog that returned with its tail between its legs* turns drama into anti-climax with the re-entry of the dog. Yet it is always possible, sometimes with a little ingenuity, to get round the problem. *The dog pursued the cat at high speed through the French windows – but it was not the cat that returned with its tail between its legs* gives an amusing twist to the sentence, with the repetition of *cat* rather than *dog* used to good effect.

While pronouns exist to relieve repetition, a sentence like *Uncle Charlie has always been one for the ladies; he has far more women friends than those who are men* makes singularly inelegant use of *those*. *Far more women than men friends* would have done the trick. The variation from *ladies* to *women* in this context is perfectly in order: lady friends, indeed, are not quite what we mean by women friends.

Which brings us to *euphemism*, elegant variation's genteel companion. Euphemism is the substitution for what the writer considers a too straightforward or harsh or unpleasant expression by a milder, inoffensive one. Euphemists do not die, they *pass away*; they do not become pregnant, they are *expecting a little stranger*; they use not the lavatory but *the smallest room*. Then there are the beg-pardon words that are not quite euphemism but which dare not speak the names of the words they represent. They do not eat, they *partake of*, and when they have partaken of, they have had not enough but *sufficient*. They use not table napkins but *serviettes*, and they *inquire*, rather than ask, if there is anything else you *require*, rather than would like.

Euphemism, in these broadminded times, is taken to less absurd lengths than when newspapers used to report *The headless body of a woman was found in Epping Forest yesterday.*

Police said she had not been interfered with. There is still a handful of sexual and scatalogical euphemisms in polite use, but latter-day euphemism is more concerned with avoiding plain speaking than with not wishing to shock. Fowler notes that the Labour Exchange has become the *Employment Exchange*; it has since become the *Job Centre*. The blind became first the *visually handicapped* and then the *visually challenged*. The United States War Department regrets not that *his parachute did not open* but that *his parachute did not achieve full deployment*; while in Cambodia an Army Air Force press officer complained to reporters, 'You always write it's bombing, bombing, bombing. It's not bombing, it's air support.' The ratcatcher, as we all tell one another, is now the *rodent operative* (although most local authorities call him the *pest control officer*).

If you are going to use euphemisms at all, then at least try to do it with style: *Beyond the garden lay a former park, common land often used for purposes better pursued in private.* Otherwise, concerning both elegant variation and euphemism, the principle to follow is to let words say what they mean. The word *dog* wants to remain a dog and not become a *hound* or *canine creature*. It does not mind being *he* or *it*. Its *supper* does not wish to be a *repast*.

Jargon

Let us agree at the outset that jargon, like sex, is all right between consenting parties. It is a form of shorthand for experts communicating only with each other, in language which to the outsider is as ancient Greek. It is when they try to impose this language on others, either because they cannot or will not translate what they have to say into plain English, or because they want to impress the layman with their expertise, that jargon is intolerable. An example is the jargon used by educators, where tests are *standard assessment tasks* and reports are *statements of attainment*. The object here seems to be to create a barrier between baffled parents and their children's teachers. The jargon of the social services – *referral, case conference, nuclear family* – and of social pressure groups – *tokenism, stereotype, workshop* – can often similarly serve to exclude outsiders.

A problem with jargon is that while it is difficult to comprehend, it is easy to compose. A junior executive programmed in office memo jargon finds it easier to write *Are all current facilities operating at their optimum efficiency or does surplus capacity exist which can be utilized?*, where the words he needs all but come out of a slot machine, than to frame a simple question: *Are you able to take on more work?* The Eurocrat, equally, finds it easy to churn out:

Member states shall presume compliance with

137

the essential requirements referred to in article 3 in respect of toys bearing the EC mark provided for in article 11 hereinafter referred to as 'EC Mark' denoting conformity with the relevant national standards which transpose the harmonized standards the reference numbers of which have been published in the Official Journal of the European Communities. Member States shall publish the reference numbers of such national standards.

The journalist Jasmine Birtles, who plucked this example of Eurospeak from the word mountain, translated it as 'If you see an EC mark on a toy it is likely to be fairly safe.' Jargon is to English what smog is to good clean air, and the way to avoid contamination is to go back to the basic idea in whatever you are writing: *rubbish dump*, not *civic amenity site*; *study the problem*, not *apply an overview to a holistic situation*; *What will this mean in terms of jobs?*, not *What are the implications for employment in the sectors mainly affected by the programme?* Have nothing to do with the jargoneer's invented vocabulary: *problemistic, non-utilization factor* (non-use) etc. Always spell out acronyms on their first appearance – not everyone knows that *GRT* means *gross registered tonnage*.

As well as the jargon of your own field, avoid the jargon of others, notably computerese: *input, feedback, software* etc. (unless you are talking about computers). Avoid, too, the buzz words and clichés that infest business English generally and which quickly lose any impact they originally had: *taken on board, customer awareness, career-motivated*. A phrase like *environment-orientated* may be passed back and forth for months without anyone ever visualizing what precisely it is supposed to mean.

Gobbledygook

While it is the aim of gobbledygook to confuse, it is not to be confused with jargon. Jargon usually has no ulterior motive beyond blinding the reader with science with a view to keeping him professionally at arm's length. Gobbledygook is meant either to disguise from the reader that the writer has little or nothing to say, or, more sinisterly, to render an unpleasant truth innocuous. *While it is not unappreciated that in a minority of instances the proposed plan, if implemented, would conceivably be contributory to some marginal inconvenience, it is nevertheless thought, after careful consideration following consultation with all interested bodies, that its benefits outweigh its peripheral disadvantages* means *Despite opposition, we are going through with the plan.* (The double negative, incidentally, is the trademark of the gobbledygooker.)

The idea of gobbledygook is often to make a simple concept seem like a complex one, thus worthy of *greater resources* (that is, more money). Gobbledygook is an American invented word, and many of its more inspired inventions are American in origin.

Correctional facility not only sanitizes the disturbing word *prison*, but it sounds altogether a grander concept, an institution in need of greater funding, research grants and so forth. Here we seem to be drifting back to euphemism: the difference is that gobbledygook has an ulterior motive. *Conference accommodation point* sounds harder to organize, and thus reflects more creditably on the organizer than mere *hotel rooms*.

Gobbledygook which says very little at great length, stretching out sentences like bubble gum, is motivated waffle, usually intended either to sell something (see any holiday brochure, or the journal which advertises itself as *a valuable multi-disciplinary current awareness resource*) or to hide something: *This guarantee does not confer any rights other than those specifically conferred above, and in particular does not cover any claims for consequential damage, but nothing contained in this guarantee shall be deemed to exclude or affect any rights which the purchaser may have apart from this guarantee*. Nothing goes fast in gobbledygook, it has a *very high speed capability*. Nowhere is quiet, it is in *a much sought-after secluded position*. Nothing is thought, it is *conceptualized*. No regrets are worth a tear, *it is a matter of regret that due to unavoidable circumstances this unfortunate situation has arisen*.

While more usually the product of low cunning, gobbledygook can sometimes be the consequence of sheer ineptitude with words. This effort from the Department of Education and Science to teachers' pay negotiators won a Golden Bull award for official gobbledy-gook from the Plain English Campaign:

> Burnham Category II/III courses may or may not be advanced and poolable. A Burnham Category II/III course which is not poolable is not poolable only because it is not advanced, i.e. it does not require course approval as an advanced course. It is therefore wrong to des-cribe it as a 'non-poolable advanced (non-designated) course.' Non-poolable courses are non-advanced by definition. I think that the problem you have described probably results from confusion here.

Gobbledygook has already a surfeit of prac-titioners. It needs no recruits.

Lifelessness

> The Grade I candidate can be expected to have demonstrated competence in deploying a range of speech styles appropriate to audience and situation and taking responsibility for or con-tributing considerably to the maintenance of an appropriate atmosphere to facilitate effective communication.

Quoting this passage in the journal *The Use of English*, its editor Roger Knight comments: 'The dulled rhythms and bureaucratic phrases that dominate this typical prescrip-tion compose a painful irony: they are unmarked by the cadences of speech, by the very essence of what they offer to describe.

Flesh and blood children don't "deploy", "maintain" and "facilitate" the living word, here neutered in the phrase "effective communication".'

Lifeless writing, as it trudges from one dead word to another, inventing its own instant jargon as it goes along, is perhaps the greatest stylistic sin of all. Lifeless writing shrinks from human contact (it is impossible to imagine the candidate quoted above as a flesh and blood person); it is frightened writing, afraid to assert itself, afraid to use commonplace words, afraid to be straightforward; speaking always in the passive voice, it dare not either raise or lower that voice for fear of breathing life into itself.

While the dead souls who write in this style may be natural bureaucrats, lifeless writing is by no means confined to the bureaucracy. It may be found in textbooks, company reports, technical papers, learned journals, military and political memoirs, even in private letters.

The way to sidestep this literary graveyard is never to forget that every piece of writing, however lofty its intention, is but the sound of one person talking to another.

Grace Notes

A piece of writing can drone or it can splutter or it can mumble or it can shout or it can sing. Aim for the singing kind – writing that has life, rhythm, harmony, style – and you will never lose your reader.

Style is nothing more nor less than the writer's voice. You have to find that voice before you can sing. These notes on style should help. Most of them summarize what has already been said in one way or another in previous sections.

Prefer short, plain words to long, college-educated ones. *End*, not *terminate*.

Use specific words, not general ones. *Coffee break*, not *interval for refreshments*.

Use concrete words, not abstract ones. *Rain*, not *inclement weather*.

Avoid abstract adjectives. *Penniless*, not *penurious*.

Prefer positive words to negative ones. *She was nineteen*, not *She was not yet twenty*.

Express even negative statements in a positive way. *He was a weak king,* not *He could not by any stretch of the imagination be called a strong ruler.*

Prefer the active voice to the passive. *His wife said nothing about the episode,* not *No mention was made of the episode.*

Do not qualify absolutes. *Impossible,* not *quite impossible.*

Do not qualify to no point. *Near,* not *pretty near.*

Use words in general use. *Solemnly affirmed,* not *asseverated.*

Do not use foreign words if you can help it. *£20,000 a year,* not *£20,000 per annum.*

Cut out superfluous words. *It is not,* not *In point of fact it is not.*

Cut out repetitive words. *Binoculars,* not *pair of binoculars.* (*Bi* means two, as in bicycle. Nobody rides a pair of bicycles, not even when they are on a tandem.) Avoid simple tautology. *Majority,* not *biggest majority.*

Do not misuse words. A *revue* is not the same as a *review.* If in doubt, check.

Take care with the formation of words. *Some of those muscle exercises make me feel thoroughly embarrassed,* not *Some of those muscle exercises make me feel thoroughly embarrassing.*

Do not propose the impossible, as in *Unless you make a will you will end up in endless trouble.*

Avoid bureaucratic verbosity. *Should the Board not approve,* not *In the event of the proposal failing to meet with the Board's approval.*

Do not use words thoughtlessly. *The Iron*

Curtain has at last risen, not *The Iron Curtain has at last come down*.

Do not (a City habit) pass verbs off as adverbs. *The level of spend* should be *The level of spending*.

Do not invent verbs. *Self-destroy*, not *self-destruct*.

Do not use nouns as verbs when they already originate from verbs. *Cross-referred*, not *cross-referenced*.

Do not stretch words out. *Dissociate*, not *disassociate*.

Do not use auxiliaries or conditionals where you do not have to. *The President is a Houdini*, not *The President is what one might call a Houdini*.

Do not use *or* as *and*. *The total of full-time and part-time students has passed all records*, not *The total of full-time or part-time students has passed all records*.

Put companion words as close as possible to each other. *Uncle Charlie's glass is empty; he has been drinking champagne and brandy*, not *Uncle Charlie's glass, out of which he has been drinking champagne and brandy, is empty*.

Put clauses in the right order to make your meaning clear. *Before going into the inn I watched a rabbit washing its face*, not *I watched a rabbit washing its face before going into the inn*.

Do not switch from one grammatical construction to another – for example, from one tense to another – in related clauses. *Every Bank Holiday he would take me to the seaside when I would always have a donkey ride*, not *Every*

Bank Holiday he would take me to the seaside when I had a donkey ride.

When dealing with the past and the present simultaneously, use the tense which controls the sentence. *Then, as now, they thought they would be able to get a job and somewhere to live*, not *Then, as now, they think they will be able* etc. But *Now, as then, they think* etc., not *Now, as then, they thought* etc.

Connect your unattached participles, even if it means demolishing and reconstructing the whole sentence. *More reminiscent of* Close Encounters of the Third Kind *than the London Underground, tunnels which do not appear on any modern map are patrolled by an inspector*, not *More reminiscent of* Close Encounters of the Third Kind, *a London Underground inspector patrols the tunnels which do not appear on any modern map.*

Do not begin a relative clause you cannot get out of (*He is the kind of man who, if he ever bought you a drink, you would never hear the last of it*), or if you do, abandon it and start again.

Keep sentence construction uniform when dealing with a list. *The army, the navy and the air force*, not *The army, the navy and air force*. Do not try to make the odd man out in a list relate to the wrong verb. *The clock is fast and unreliable and it chimes only every two hours*, not *The clock is fast, unreliable and chimes only every two hours.*

Put the emphasis in the right place. Either *Last night, his courageous battle over, he died* or *He died last night, his courageous battle over*, not

His courageous battle over, he died last night.

Do not over-punctuate, but never fail to supply the closing comma in a parenthetical phrase marked off by commas. *The hotel, while only fifteen minutes by car from the city centre, is in the heart of the country*, not *The hotel, while only fifteen minutes by car from the city centre is in the heart of the country.*

If, after all this advice, a sentence still reads awkwardly, then what you have there is an awkward sentence. Demolish it and start again.